THE FIVE MARKS OF A MAN
DEVOTIONAL

THE FIVE MARKS OF A MAN
DEVOTIONAL

60 DAYS TO A POWERFUL LIFE

BRIAN TOME

BakerBooks

a division of Baker Publishing Group
Grand Rapids, Michigan

© 2024 by Brian Tome

Published by Baker Books
a division of Baker Publishing Group
Grand Rapids, Michigan
BakerBooks.com

Printed in China

Library of Congress Cataloging-in-Publication Data
Names: Tome, Brian, author.
Title: The five marks of a man devotional : 60 days to a powerful life / Brian Tome.
Description: Grand Rapids, Michigan : Baker Books, a division of Baker Publishing
    Group, [2024] | Devotional companion to Five marks of a man / Brian Tome. Grand
    Rapids, Michigan : Baker Books, a division of Baker Publishing Group, [2018]. |
    Includes bibliographical references.
Identifiers: LCCN 2024005424 | ISBN 9781540903143 (paper) | ISBN
    9781493445776 (ebook)
Subjects: LCSH: Christian men—Prayers and devotions. | Devotional literature. |
    Christian men—Conduct of life. | Christian men—Religious life.
Classification: LCC BV4528.2 .T662 2024 | DDC 248.8/42—dc23/eng/20240328
LC record available at https://lccn.loc.gov/2024005424

Cover design by Crossroads

Published in association with The Bindery Agency, LLC, www.TheBinderyAgency.com.

Baker Publishing Group publications use paper produced from sustainable forestry practices and postconsumer waste whenever possible.

24   25   26   27   28   29   30   7   6   5   4   3   2   1

CONTENTS

WEEK 5

WEEK 6

WEEK 7

WEEK 8

WEEK 9

WEEK 10

WEEK 11

WEEK 12

INTRODUCTION

If you read introductions, you are a better man than me. But my publisher says we need one, so here goes.

Because you have picked up this book, I believe I know something about you. No one picks up a devotional book looking to just pass the time. You are here because you want something more. You desire a life that isn't frail and flimsy. You are looking for meaningfulness and weightiness. I believe, like many men, you are chasing gravitas.

In space, and in life, objects with more mass draw the less weighty things into their orbit. Gravitas (or gravity) pulls the moon into orbit around the earth, just like the much more massive sun draws the earth.

Do you want that for your life? Do you want a sort of X factor that brings a weight to your life and words?

Godly gravitas comes from a deep and abiding relationship with God through his Son, Jesus. You develop that relationship by getting to know God and doing the things that separate men from boys.

Boys don't have gravitas. They float from one thing to the next, as light as a feather in a windstorm. Men, on the other hand, have a weight. They are sturdy, dependable, and hold the line.

I didn't know it at the time, but I struggled to become a man. Well into my twenties and beyond, I continued to live like a boy, mostly because I didn't know any better. Like most people, I thought age was what separated the men from the boys. You are a boy until you are eighteen years old, then you can smoke and register for military service, so that makes you a man. Wrong.

Other people I know think it is a job that separates the men from the boys. Getting a corner office or climbing the ladder or at least having enough income to buy a house and a cool car is what finally marks you as a man. Wrong.

Some people think you cross into manhood after your first time having sex. Wrong. Or when you get married. Also wrong. Or when you have kids. Wrong again.

When I seriously started to follow Jesus and committed my life to doing ministry full-time, I managed to beat back many of my boyish tendencies. With each small victory I gained some gravitas. But even this did not mark me as a man. I know successful pastors of large churches who still haven't grown into manhood. And no, I won't tell you their names.

When my son was born, I knew I had to wrestle this to the ground. If I didn't want him to repeat the sins of his father— being a terror, using up resources until they were depleted, living a self-focused, me-first life—I needed a model to point him toward.

As I examined the lives of every man I considered great, from heroes of the Bible to my own mentors and father figures, five different marks started to emerge. These were the traits that gave them gravitas.

The weighty men that I wanted to be like had *vision*. They set their lives toward things that were more than just having a good day. They put in the reps, day in and day out, to make it a reality.

These men took *minority positions*, swimming upstream to do what was unpopular but right. It was a minority position to give their time and influence to a punk kid like me, but it was a decision that changed my life.

The men I most wanted to emulate were all *team players*. In a world awash in solo MVPs, these men worked for championship trophies, not individual stats. In varying ways, they each "lost" as individuals so their teams could win.

These men were driven by a strong *work ethic*. Whether it was working at their nine-to-five, doing house projects for their families on the weekends, or giving up their free nights to lead student ministries, they worked hard at everything they did.

The men I admired were all *protectors*. When I was with them, I felt safe—not just physically but also relationally, spiritually, and even financially. I am at the place I am in my life today because of heavyweight champion men who have protected me and my family—from words of encouragement spoken at just the right moment to bags of groceries to physical needs when my home burned down as a young family man.

I saw the same attributes on display in spiritual greats like Abraham and Joseph, David and Elijah, Peter and Paul, and especially in the life of Christ. We will get into all those specifics as you work through this book.

Near the end of 1 Corinthians, a letter Paul wrote to a church that he loved, he gives his readers some interesting advice:

> Be watchful, stand firm in the faith, act like men, be strong. Let all that you do be done in love. (1 Cor. 16:13–14)

In those two verses, Paul sets up the parameters that, for me, became the five marks.

"Be watchful"—Men have a vision.

"Stand firm in the faith"—There's no need to stand firm unless you are standing against the tide. Men take minority positions.

"Act like men"—Notice this command is written in the plural. Manhood isn't an individual journey. Men are team players.

"Be strong"—Men understand they are wired to produce value, something that requires strength and determination. Men work.

"Let all you do be done in love"—You don't do things "in love" for yourself but for others. Men are protectors.

As I researched and expounded on the five marks, I found more than just my own family was helped. I introduced them in sermons and live speaking events everywhere from fraternities at secular universities to NFL locker rooms. The feedback was more than I could have anticipated. Men were helped, women found clarity about the men in their lives, and families were changed. The five marks were put into book form, and the rest is history.

Years after the first publication of *The Five Marks of a Man*, the book continues to make waves. That is why you hold this devotional in your hands. It is not an easy money grab or an attempt to hit the *New York Times* bestseller list (though I wouldn't hate that) or an effort to fulfill some contractual obligation. Time and sweat and effort built this book because the five marks work best on a spiritual foundation.

Nearly every morning of the year (I said *nearly*—I'm not perfect at this either), I spend time reading Scripture and praying. Oftentimes, I will peck out some thoughts on my phone, responding to the Scripture that I've read. They show up in a spiritual fitness app developed by some smart cookies at the church I pastor. (It's called Crossroads Any-where. It's free and you are welcome to join thousands of other people using it to build their spiritual fitness.) On the app, users can publish and read journal entries, pray for each other, practice gratitude, and more.

But it's not just reading the Bible that creates a spiritual foundation to build your life upon—you actually have to do what it says. This book is designed to push you to do both.

Each entry in this devotional book starts with a Scripture. After that, you'll find some of my thoughts about it, many of which started as journal entries in that spiritual fitness app. After that is a short prayer in my own words, though you are always welcome to adjust it to fit you.

Most importantly, each day ends with a section called "Get in the Game." Don't skip this. These prompts are designed to push you to not just read the Bible but work its wisdom into your everyday life. Choose *one* of the prompts and get to moving. Your life doesn't advance just by thinking the right thoughts. If you want something different, you have to do something different.

If you are still reading this, you obviously don't need guidance on how to read. But the publishers say clarity is best. I promise, we are almost done here.

This book is divided into twelve weeks. Each week contains five devotional entries, one for each of the five marks. Every week you will be pushed to have a vision, take minority positions, be a team player, work hard, and live as a protector. In that order. Again and again and again.

This was done intentionally, because driving a nail takes more than one whack with a weighty hammer. While a finishing nail might be put into place with two or three hammer swings, a railroad spike takes many more.

Building a powerful life requires hit after hit after hit. It takes consistency. It takes intentionality. It takes healthy aggressiveness, defaulting toward movement instead of passivity. The more you practice each of the marks, the more you will naturally find them present in your life. More than just completing a book, you are laying down rails for your life to run on.

About this time, I expect the anal-retentive people in the back to raise their hands and remind us that a week actually has seven days. Correct. In this book, our weeks have five days. Free days, missed days, and off days are built in. You are welcome.

This is a choose your own adventure. You can begin day 1 on a Monday and do one entry for each day of the workweek, taking Saturday and Sunday off. If you do it this way, this book will take approximately three months to get through.

Or you can go pedal to the floor and do one entry a day with no breaks. If you do that, you'll finish in two months.

For an added boost, work through this book alongside other guys you respect. Talk about what you are learning, support each other through the "Get in the Game" challenges, and laugh over drinks on a regular basis. This will make the experience all the more powerful.

This book is a tool, so don't try to keep it pristine. Dog-ear the pages. Use the checkboxes on the table of contents. Circle things you want to remember, draw a line through things you think are stupid. Scuff it up and make it yours.

No matter how you use this book, know that it follows a rhythm, and every five days you will begin that rhythm again. Each week is a blow from a hammer that is driving a stake into the ground.

You are a man, and you are capable of living a powerful life alongside a God who designed you to do just that. He is for you. He actually enjoys your sense of humor. He wants to spend time with you. He is rooting for you, and so am I.

Enough locker-room talk. Let's get to the weight room.

It's time to grow some gravitas.

WEEK

1

DAY 1

TIME TO GET MOVING
MEN HAVE A VISION

> But understand this, that in the last days there will come
> times of difficulty. For people will be lovers of self, lovers of
> money, proud, arrogant, abusive, disobedient to their par-
> ents, ungrateful, unholy, . . . always learning and never able
> to arrive at a knowledge of the truth.
>
> 2 Timothy 3:1–2, 7

We live in a culture of endless learning opportunities. The
upside is that the information superhighway can answer
any question you throw at it. With a click of a button you
can start a side hustle, book a vacation home, or learn to
rebuild the engine of a 1978 Jeep CJ7—sometimes even
all at once.

The downside is that we learn things without actually doing
things. Our world is full of information and short on action.

I see this with spiritual seekers who perpetually seek but
never find. Instead of clasping and grabbing hold of what

they find, they move from one thing to the next in a seemingly endless cycle. They are like baby birds with open mouths who never shut them, swallow, digest, and grow.

This is also a problem with believers who think that gaining more knowledge is the key to spiritual growth. No, it's doing what you already know that leads to spiritual breakthrough and the advancement of God's kingdom.

I know people who get frustrated at the church I lead because we don't offer enough classes to help them "go to the next level." I'm not exactly sure what they mean by that, and I'm not sure they do either. Chasing knowledge for the sake of knowledge is like trying to catch the wind. Just when you think you've grabbed it, you'll find it slipping away again.

We've become like people I know who are perpetually in school without having a successful career. Eventually you get the PhD but feel lost. Education is only meant to get you a job so that you can do something. We don't see Jesus with his disciples, Paul with Timothy, or anyone in the book of Acts modeling or teaching that more information is the key to growth.

When I read Scripture, I constantly remind myself that I'm not trying to accomplish a reading goal. I'm wanting to know God better so I can move. I'm not trying to just fill my head with more knowledge. If I never learn anything else in the Bible (which isn't likely), I'm confident I already know enough to go on for the rest of my life.

It's likely you don't need to learn anything else either—at least not to take the first step. We can treat knowledge like insurance, getting more and more to try to cushion our lives against uncertainty and risk. But that will only keep you stalled.

A vision is a call to action, while perpetual learning and research is a stalling technique. You likely already know everything you need to chase the vision God has in front of you for today.

Stop learning and start acting. Step by step, that's how every vision gets accomplished.

Prayer

God, I'm sorry for times I haven't acted on your promptings and visions in the past. I do not want to hide on the sidelines waiting for more knowledge. I want to be in the game. I commit to taking a step, however small, toward a vision today. Amen.

Get in the Game

1. Do you have a vision that's become more of an intellectual pursuit than a physical one? Welcome to the club. Think of one thing you can do today to push that vision ahead—and go do it.

      OR

2. Don't know what vision to chase? Ask God to give you a vision. Then spend five minutes in silence just listening. If a thought enters your mind, assume it's from God. Make the first move on it today.

DAY 2

STARTING SMALL
MEN TAKE MINORITY POSITIONS

> Then [Jesus] began to denounce the cities where most
> of his mighty works had been done, because they did not
> repent. "Woe to you, Chorazin! Woe to you, Bethsaida! For
> if the mighty works done in you had been done in Tyre and
> Sidon, they would have repented long ago in sackcloth and
> ashes."
>
> Matthew 11:20–21

Last year, I got to travel to Germany. Part of my experiences
there included touring the Nazi concentration camp at Buchenwald. It was an appropriately weighty and heavy experience, and it is not something I will soon forget.

Everywhere I turned, I saw signs of a culture that again and
again chose the wrong path. As the Nazis rose to power,
there were precious few people willing to take the minority
position to stand against the rising tide that would do so
much damage.

Walking out of Buchenwald, I couldn't help but wonder how I would have responded if I were a German in the 1930s and 40s. Would I have toed the line with the masses, keeping quiet out of self-preservation? Would I have gone the opposite way and put my life, and the lives of my family, on the line?

The way to know if we would have been faithful back then is to ask if we are being faithful right now.

Jesus had higher expectations for the people closest to him. He spoke out against Chorazin and Bethsaida because they had seen things and knew things that other cities never got the chance to experience, yet they still persisted in their old ways. They refused to repent, which is a word that simply means to "change direction."

Like those cities, I've also seen things, experienced things, and known things that others haven't. When I persist in choosing the wrong path, I'm not just going the way of the masses and walking with the misguided majority—I'm closing my eyes to all God has done and said in my life in the past. He takes this personally.

Jesus taught that faithfulness in big things comes only after being faithful in small things (Luke 16:10). I can daydream about how I would have responded to the Nazis, but it's a better use of my time to look for ways to be faithful in the small things God puts in front of me today.

Building muscle in small minority positions today will make it easier to take larger ones in the future.

Aim to start small today, being faithful in whatever God puts in front of you.

Prayer

Jesus, I don't want to be like the faithless cities you called on the carpet. Remind me of the things from you I have seen and experienced, and open my eyes to a minority position I need to take today. I want to be faithful in the small things so I can be trusted with big things. Amen.

Get in the Game

1. Engage a small minority position today to build muscle for larger ones later. If you already know what you're going to do, then get to it. If you don't, ask God to put one in front of you, then go about your day with muscles primed to move.

    OR

2. Open your calendar app and scroll back a few months. What have you seen, experienced, or learned recently that you need to reengage today? Do that and push back against the faithlessness of the majority who live blind to what God is doing.

DAY 3

GRAB A SHOVEL
MEN ARE TEAM PLAYERS

> Where there are no oxen, the manger is clean,
> but abundant crops come by the strength of the ox.
>
> Proverbs 14:4

If you want to have a transcendent life, you will need good people around you. Like the oxen in this proverb, people will need to eat. And then they'll need to crap. Being a team player means raising your hand and saying, "I'm willing to grab a shovel and get to scooping."

If you are married and don't want any mess, don't have kids. If you are a business owner and don't want any tension, don't try to grow your reach. If you want a sane and manageable life, don't invest your time into spiritually parenting others. If you want a perfectly predictable calendar, don't invite other people into your days.

But if you want abundant crops, you are going to need oxen—not to work for you but to pull with you. While oxen are slower than horses, they're stronger, can endure more, and will last longer. While one ox can pull 3,000 pounds alone, two oxen yoked together can pull as much as 12,000 to 13,000 pounds.[1] The uptick is exponential.

Oxen will eat. A quick Google search says a single ox can eat thirty pounds of hay a day—more if it is working hard.[2]

Being a team player means "feeding" your team. That might mean grabbing an actual meal together. It can also mean sending an encouraging text, grabbing a drink on someone's birthday, or just calling to check in. Well-fed oxen are healthier, just like friends who feel seen and appreciated are a greater joy to be around.

When oxen eat, they will eventually crap. A mature ox can produce 65 to 80 pounds of poop every day.[3] People in your life will do the same. There will be complications, conflict, and mess. Sometimes you'll find yourself at the center of it, and other times you'll be on the outside. Either way, you'll need to grab your shovel.

I don't know why we keep thinking that life should be easier. All living things produce waste. The only way my life would be easier would be if I chose to be lifeless and alone. That's not how I want to live. I don't want easy and sane, I want lasting impact. I don't want buttoned-up and clean, I want authentic. I don't want a shiny veneer, I want vibrant abundance.

My fantasy of living off the grid in a mountain cabin might mean less crap to shovel, but it would also be boring and meaningless.

Whatever interpersonal issues I'm having to deal with today, I choose to see them as a blessing. It means God has given me friends and family to fight for. He has counted me worthy to handle a shovel and move some crap.

It's time to get to it.

Prayer

God, your wisdom is unmatched. It is practical and applicable. I am sorry for thinking the people in my life aren't worth the effort. If you have blessed me with friends, I commit to feeding and cleaning up after them today. If I can't name anyone on my team, I commit to taking steps to change that today. Amen.

Get in the Game

1. *Feeding.* When was the last time you made a significant investment into your friends or family? Ask God who needs some of your time and attention today, then do it. You might choose to take a friend to lunch, toss a football with your kids, go on a walk with your spouse after work, or something else.

   OR

2. *Shoveling.* Is there a relationship mess or conflict you need to address? Ask God what it means for you to grab your shovel and start scooping, then get to it. The longer you wait to address issues, the more difficult and complicated they will become. Act today.

DAY 4

THE RIGHT TO FIGHT
MEN WORK

> See, I have set the land before you. Go in and take possession of the land that the LORD swore to your fathers, to Abraham, to Isaac, and to Jacob, to give to them and to their offspring after them.
>
> Deuteronomy 1:8

Not that I am qualified to adjust the words of the Bible, but I wish God would have chosen to use a word other than "give" in this verse and many others like it. When I think of something being given to me, I think of passively receiving a gift, something I don't have to work to receive. God does give in that way, but not in this case.

Some five hundred years earlier, God had entered into a deal with a man named Abraham. If Abraham would leave his homeland and follow God to a new place, God promised to give that land to him and his descendants.

In Deuteronomy 1:8, Abraham's descendants, the nation of Israel, now stood on the edge of this promised land. God was ready to give it to them, but there would be nothing passive about it. Instead, Israel was being given the right to fight giants, conquer cities, crisscross hundreds of miles on foot, and have a percentage of their people die in order to take and settle their promised land. After the battles, their future would be one of building homes, planting and harvesting crops, and raising livestock. In short, they would have to work for it.

They would ultimately be grateful for that privilege, but not before some difficult times. When spies ventured into the land, they came back with reports of how difficult the war campaign would be. The fears grew like a flame in the wind, spreading throughout the nation as nearly everyone became immobilized by fear and lost their faith. They wouldn't cross the line into the promised land, so God turned them around. They then had to wander for forty more years until the faithless and powerless people died and the rest of the nation was ready to work and fight for God's promises.

I see people grow frustrated with God because they aren't being given something that seems to be part of his will and vision for their life. But are we willing to fight for it? If you want to get out of debt, are you fighting for it by working a budget, eating oatmeal, and skipping the Starbucks run every morning? If you want to be married, are you working on your dysfunctions, your communication ability, and getting out from behind your game console in preparation for being an actual teammate? If you want better health, are you hitting the gym, making wise food choices, and getting adequate rest? If you want to hear from God, are you spending time with him?

We love to hear the promises of God, but it is the minority of men who opt in to backbreaking labor to secure them. We've been deluded into thinking if God has given something to us, it will fall into our lap. Not so. When God gives, he gives permission for us to go after it—to fight and take the land before us.

Prayer

Lord, you haven't called me to a life of ease. You've called me to work. I don't want to sit idle on the sidelines, I want to be in the fight. Show me an opportunity to move toward your promises and plans today, and I vow to put in the hard work. Amen.

Get in the Game

1. Where in your life are you passively waiting for things to change—finances, relationships, work, your health? Take the fight to it today. Choose one positively aggressive move and do it in the next twenty-four hours.

   OR

2. When Moses sent the twelve spies into the promised land, he sent them in pairs. Only one pair remained faithful. Think of someone you know who is attempting to take new land in their life. Shoot them a text message of encouragement right now to keep going.

DAY 5

DEFENSE AND OFFENSE
MEN ARE PROTECTORS

> Blessed be the LORD, my rock,
>   who trains my hands for war,
>   and my fingers for battle.
>
> Psalm 144:1

Life is a fight. We need high ground for defense and skill for offense.

The ground beneath our feet doesn't matter much until we're called to defend it. When we are in a fight, what we're standing on matters. In high school football, trying to hold a block on a wet and muddy field is a challenge. Trying to hold your ground in water or on ice is even more difficult.

God is a rock I stand and build my life upon. He is the high ground that is unchanging and relentless. He has never been overpowered and he will not start now.

But God isn't content with just a solid defense. He trains our hands for war, our fingers for battle, and he sends us out into the fray.

Most people would rather be trained for peace and solace. They prefer an easy day to a challenging one, a life of passive defense instead of aggressive offense. I am one of them. I like peace and solace as much as the next guy. Scripture like this reorients my vision. I am reminded that vacation days are the exception, not the rule.

If we aren't training for war, we will fall every time. Psalm 144 was written by David, Israel's greatest king and a man very familiar with combat. Battle in David's day wasn't flying a drone with your thumbs or launching missiles from hundreds of miles away. It was hand-to-hand combat with a twenty-five-pound sword and a bow strung with the tendons of a deer. If you didn't have hands trained in skill, strength, and endurance, you weren't going to last long.

There are not a lot of people who have skill in disarming the enemy, let alone strength and endurance. We've grown soft. We've lost our penchant for conflict. We would rather drop our sword than grip it. Our fingers are not seasoned enough to handle a battle bow. When things get hard, we complain about how unfair life is, blame God, and run for cover. We need to remember, that's just how battle is. It is intense, demanding, and dangerous.

Men recognize that life is a fight and that God has trained them as active participants—we are the protectors.

Men protect physically, using their strength and cunning to disarm and minimize threats against the most vulnerable. Men protect spiritually, prayerfully putting themselves on the line to help others grow and thrive. Men protect relationally, guarding the emotions and well-being of the people who depend on them. Men protect financially, saving and spending so that others are blessed.

God is our defense. He is training and deploying us as the offensive force in his world. Today, let's take new ground.

Prayer

Lord, thank you for being my fortress and my rock. The way you have constantly protected me sets an example for me to follow. However you want to train my hands for war today, I am all in. I will not run from the battles you set before me. Amen.

Get in the Game

1. Drop to the ground and do as many push-ups as you can right now. Feel the tension in your chest and triceps as each push-up gets harder. This is what training feels like. When you feel tension as a protector today, see it as training and lean into it. God is forming you.

   OR

2. Men protect on four fronts: physically, spiritually, relationally, and financially. Which one do you see as your strongest? Which one do you see as your weakest? Now pray about it. Thank God for the ways he has trained you in your strength, and ask him for an opportunity to be trained in your weakest area today. Look for that training, and take the first opportunity that comes your way.

WEEK
2

DAY 6

MAKING PEACE WITH PAIN
MEN HAVE A VISION

For you yourselves know that we are destined for this. For when we were with you, we kept telling you beforehand that we were to suffer affliction, just as it has come to pass, and just as you know.

1 Thessalonians 3:3–4

Scholars believe that Paul wrote his first letter to the Thessalonian church, including these still-hard-to-read words, about fifteen years after he became a follower of Jesus. It echoes some of the first words he received after encountering Christ.

Originally a persecutor of the start-up church, Paul met Jesus in a vision while on his way to Damascus to arrest and kill believers. He was blinded by the encounter, and God spoke to a man named Ananias, instructing him to go and pray for Paul's sight to be restored. God told Ananias that Paul was his "chosen instrument to proclaim my name to the Gentiles and their kings and to the people of Israel. I will show him how much he must suffer for my name" (Acts 9:15–16 NIV).

Suffering isn't a vision any of us would pick for our lives, but a decade and a half in, Paul has made peace with it. This is one of the reasons his life works. Paul has accepted something most of us still push against: that every vision from God will be met with difficulty, complexity, and adversity.

Why do we think that knowing Jesus means not knowing hardship? Following Christ means going in a different direction than we were originally headed. It means going against cultural norms, family patterns, and long-held expectations. It means going somewhere we otherwise wouldn't go. If difficulty and suffering were par for the course for Christ, and if we're following him, why should we expect our experience to be any different?

I know many people who are "deconstructing" their faith. For most of them, that's just another way of saying "leaving." A common denominator among most people I know in that situation is that life got difficult. More difficult than they thought was fair. More difficult than it should be if God were real and cared.

He is real and he does care . . . AND he also uses difficulty to form us. The great apostle Paul, who had one of the most potent and powerful lives in history, was called by God into a life of suffering. This is too much for most of us because we have the wrong motive for faith. We think God exists to make our lives better and easier. Not true. We exist to bring God's will to fruition. This is hard work. Paul had an incredibly meaningful life . . . and it also included learning to find joy in the midst of hardship.

That doesn't mean that I look forward to difficult days. I don't. But it does mean that I expect them to come, so when they do, I'm not shaken or tempted to throw in the towel.

We must not shrink back from challenges and difficulty. Any vision worth following will include plenty of both.

The sooner we make peace with pain, the more resilient we (and our visions) will become.

Prayer

Father, forgive me for thinking you have abandoned me in times of adversity. I trust you are using them to deepen our relationship and bring about your will. I recommit myself to follow you and your visions through muck and mire and to not give up so easily. Amen.

Get in the Game

1. Are you experiencing difficulty around a vision you are chasing?

   If so, be encouraged. That means you're actually moving on it. Pray and ask God to meet you in that difficulty and to help you weather it like the spiritual greats.

   If not, it likely means your vision is either stalled or too small. Put the ball into the field of play today by making an intentional move toward your vision. If difficulty comes because of it, take it as encouragement and keep moving forward.

   OR

2. Build muscle for the next round of difficulty by purposefully introducing some difficulty into your day.

Pick something challenging and then do it to help yourself make peace with pain. Choose your own adventure or pick one of the following:

- Take the stairs all day.

- Park in the back of the parking lot.

- Clean out the workroom fridge at the office.

- Pay for someone else's groceries.

- Lift weights or go for a challenging run.

DAY 7

A SPIRITUAL SELF-DIAGNOSTIC
MEN TAKE MINORITY POSITIONS

> But if we judged ourselves truly, we would not be judged.
> But when we are judged by the Lord, we are disciplined so
> that we may not be condemned along with the world.
>
> 1 Corinthians 11:31–32

Matthew 7:1, "Judge not, that you be not judged," has to
be the most misquoted verse in the entire Bible. It's used
daily by believers and atheists alike, usually to sidestep the
consequences of a mistake or a questionable choice.

Culture loves that verse because it feels like a get-out-of-
jail-free card. But that's completely missing Jesus's point.
He isn't telling us not to be discerning. He isn't telling us
not to be wise or perceptive or discriminating. He is merely
reminding us that God is God and we are not. There is
always more going on behind the scenes than we can ever

know or understand. Our judgments of others are nearly always shortsighted.

The minority position is to take our judgmental eye and point it inward. It is there that I may discover something that I need to change about my own life. This rubs against the majority opinion of looking outward, finding something bad about someone else so that we can feel superior. When we learn to spend our energy critiquing ourselves instead of others, our lives go to the next level.

When I am feeling down or when life doesn't seem to be working, the first thing I do is run a self-diagnostic. Are there areas in my life where I'm rebelling against God? Are there secret sins I'm hiding? Am I quick at doing the things God wants me to do, or am I dragging my feet? Am I being generous? Am I being forgiving? Am I pushing myself to serve others?

When our tires are out of alignment with each other, the car will pull and shake. Likewise, when our life is out of alignment with God, we will experience an uncomfortable pulling and shaking.

Being down, or having a life that isn't all up and to the right, does not always mean we are out of alignment. Sometimes life is just hard, and there can be long seasons where it sucks. But doing an honest spiritual self-check is a simple first step to kick-starting growth. Simple because it is doable, not easy.

Honestly judging ourselves can be a painful experience. But like Paul explains in today's Scripture, either we can judge ourselves and fix problems before they get out of hand, or we can wait to be disciplined by the Lord. I know which one I'd rather do.

Time to run another self-check.

Prayer

Father, I am sorry for how easy it is for me to judge others. I want to learn to turn that gaze inward so that I remain in perfect alignment with you. If anything is off, let me know and I will fix it today. Amen.

Get in the Game

1. King David wrote out one of his self-diagnostic prayers in Psalm 139:23–24. Read it, and if you are serious about getting into alignment with God, pray it for yourself. Then take some time to listen for God's response. If something pops into your mind, assume it's from him and act on it today.

   OR

2. Even when things seem to be going well, a spiritual checkup is always a good idea. Open your calendar app and set a reminder for six months from today to do this exercise again.

DAY 8

THE MOST IMPORTANT GIFT
MEN ARE TEAM PLAYERS

While he was in one of the cities, there came a man full of leprosy. And when he saw Jesus, he fell on his face and begged him, "Lord, if you will, you can make me clean." And Jesus stretched out his hand and touched him, saying, "I will; be clean." And immediately the leprosy left him. And he charged him to tell no one, but "go and show yourself to the priest, and make an offering for your cleansing."

Luke 5:12–14

In this passage, Jesus heals a man with a serious skin disease. While it looks like the most significant change coming out of this interaction is physical, it's actually not. The most important gift Jesus was giving this man was a return to relationships.

In the first century, leprosy was a physical and relational death sentence. The brutal skin disease had no known cure and was highly contagious. Lepers were driven out of town, away from their friends and family, and forced to live together in ramshackle colonies. They weren't welcome in the temple, in the marketplace, or at their jobs. They were openly reviled. Lepers were forced to scratch together a living, oftentimes begging for food. As the disease progressed, victims were known to lose limbs and become horribly disfigured, only adding to their isolation.

Leprosy was so horrible, it was commonly assumed that anyone who contracted the disease was being punished by God. This man who approaches Jesus has significant pain points on every level: physical, relational, emotional, and spiritual. Aside from any other lepers he might spend time with, he is essentially an island unto himself. No one would dare give him the time of day—except for the Son of God.

Jesus heals the man by touching him. The man must have been startled after going months, maybe even years, without any physical interaction from another human. But then Jesus does something that seems odd: he tells the man not to spread the news but to go straight to the priest.

Why? Jesus is pointing him to the biggest gift. In the Jewish law of the Old Testament, there was only one way for a leper to be welcomed back into the community: a priest had to vouch for him that he was cured. After that, the exile of leprosy would be over. Jesus doesn't want the fame and accolades that a legit miracle could bring him. He wants this man to get to rebuilding his relational life.

I have said it many times, but it is worth repeating. If I could give one spiritual discipline to every man I know, it wouldn't be consistent Bible reading, prayer, or church attendance. All those things are good and very important. What I would give them is friendship. Men are lonely, suffering, and adrift. That's because so many of us aren't running beside other good men. We may not have leprosy, but we are experiencing isolation. Jesus wants none of it.

Jesus set this man free from illness, then pushed him out of isolation. I believe he is doing the same for you because he wants more for you. Wolves need a pack in order to survive and thrive. Power comes in community. Lone wolves are weaker than those in a pack and die sooner. The same will be said of us if we don't break out of the American delusion that men should be rugged individualists who don't need anybody.

Men are team players. If you don't have a team, it's time to start looking for one. If you do have one, it's time to reconnect.

Let's leave the isolation of the leper colony behind. Jesus wants you to have friends. It's time to find your pack.

Prayer

Jesus, like the man you healed, I understand that you have created me for relationships. I am sorry for the times I choose isolation instead. It might be easier, but it is not better. Whether I have significant friendships or not, today I choose to take a step toward that most important gift. You are good to give it to me and to push me further. I will follow. Amen.

Get in the Game

1. If your friendships aren't up to snuff, you aren't alone. The most recent statistics say one out of every six men has no friends,[1] and a little less than 50 percent of all men are not satisfied with the level of friendships they currently have.[2] Those statistics won't change on their own. Spend a few minutes asking God to examine your friendships (or lack thereof) and to give you an idea of how you can take action today. The first thing that pops into your head and that you think Jesus would approve of is your task. Go and do it.

   OR

2. Adult friendships take initiative, and male friendships are most often based around shared experiences. This week, invite a guy you enjoy spending time with to do something with you—go kayaking, get tickets to a football game, smoke meat in the backyard, or tour a local brewery. Even if a deep friendship doesn't form, you have shown God you value relationships, and this will please him.

DAY 9

GOD IS INVESTED
MEN WORK

> Whatever you do, work heartily, as for the Lord
> and not for men.
>
> Colossians 3:23

This verse was one that I drilled into my kids, but it is just as meaningful for me now as it was thirty years ago. Every aspect of everything I do today is an opportunity to serve God—even at my nine-to-five. Actually, especially at my nine-to-five. Adam and Eve were placed on the earth to work and experience God before anything wrong took place (Gen. 2:15). We can do the same.

The statistics paint a clear picture: Americans are nowhere near "working heartily."

In North America, only 31 percent of employees report being engaged in their workplace, meaning they are enthusiastic and involved in their work and its success. The remaining 69 percent were either not engaged (52 percent) or actively disengaged (17 percent).[1]

On average, nearly 85 percent of people report being distracted at work. The most common culprits are calls and texts (55 percent), the internet (41 percent), other coworkers (27 percent), and email (26 percent).[2] All those distractions add up to a company loss of 720 hours a year per employee—or about one-third of their entire working hours.[3]

Nearly six in ten employees qualify as quiet quitters. They might show up to work physically but are psychologically disengaged, leading to a significant drop in productivity.[4]

Colossians 3:23 is a wake-up call for a disengaged culture. Whether you run payroll spreadsheets, wire houses, or flip burgers, your work matters because you are working for God.

When you see payroll as assisting God in taking care of his children by making sure they get their wages, your attitude will change. When you understand that wiring houses blesses people in your community with a safe place to live, it adjusts your perspective. When you get the picture that the burger you just prepared is taking something off the plate of a busy and committed mother, you'll keep flipping.

God is invested in my work. He cares about how many hours I put in today. He cares about my energy in meetings. He cares about my demeanor around the office or worksite. He cares whether I am giving my full attention to others by looking them in the eye or already looking over their shoulder to the next thing. He cares about how I represent my company. He cares about my follow-through and reliability.

God wants me fully engaged all forty-ish hours this week. When I'm phoning it in or distracted, he takes it personally. That doesn't mean I'll never change jobs, but it does mean that I'll give my best today. I don't work for a paycheck, and I don't work to accumulate accolades from my manager. I work to please God.

It's easy to understand that God cares about how I spend my off-hours with family and friends. Understanding that he equally cares about my work and that my work ethic reflects what I think about him compels me to "work heartily."

Work is an act of worship every bit as spiritual as singing a chorus at church or reading my Bible. I will give it my all today.

Prayer

God, I want my work to bring you honor today. When I am tempted to give less than my best, remind me that whatever I am doing, I am doing it for you. You are worth every effort and more. Amen.

Get in the Game

1. Look ahead to your next workday (check your calendar app if you need to). Identify everything you will do and spend time connecting each task with a tangible blessing for God or other people. (Example: manufacturing cars blesses people with transportation; working in HR is taking care of God's people). Carry this perspective into your next workday and pay attention to how it adjusts your attitude.

   OR

2. The next time you commute to work (in the car, on a bus, or making the walk from your kitchen table to a home office), listen to worship music. Use the commute time as a reminder that God considers the next eight hours at work an opportunity for worship. Now get out there and crush it.

DAY 10

THE BEST HAVE BRUISES
MEN ARE PROTECTORS

> And they said, "Is not this Joseph's son?" And he said to them, "Doubtless you will quote to me this proverb, '"Physician, heal yourself." What we have heard you did at Capernaum, do here in your hometown as well.'"
>
> Luke 4:22–23

"Physician, heal yourself" was a popular saying of the day, similar to our saying "The cobbler's children have no shoes." It means, "You are helping other people, so how about helping those closest to you?"

Jesus grew up in the town of Nazareth but had adopted the village of Capernaum as his home base for ministry. This interaction in Luke 4 happens on his first return trip to Nazareth after buzz about him starts to spread. The people who knew him as a child and teenager are wanting in on the action. They want to see what their hometown boy can do.

I sense cynicism in their request, like the leaders of Nazareth are taunting Jesus. They are saying, "You did cool stuff elsewhere—how about doing some for us now?" They also make a jab about Joseph, Jesus's father. They don't believe Jesus had a divine beginning in the womb of his virgin mother, Mary. This is just another example that Jesus's life wasn't buttoned-up and perfect. He was perfect in relation to sin, but that doesn't mean he didn't experience relational turbulence.

Here are just a few examples that we know of . . .

- Jesus was born into financial poverty. Many scholars believe the gifts he received from the wise men would have been sold to help pay for the early years of his life.

- He lived under the constant rumor and hushed accusation that Joseph wasn't his real dad and that he was a bastard. You can almost hear the sneer in their voices when they say, "Is not this Joseph's son?"

- Earlier in Luke 4, Jesus experienced forty days of suffering in the wilderness with no food or water and going head-to-head with Satan.

- In the end, he had three of the worst days in recorded history. He was abandoned by everyone, rejected so that a murderer (Barabbas) could go free, and then publicly put to death in the most painful way possible.

- The final jab came on the cross, when an actual criminal being crucified alongside him taunted him with "You saved others, but you can't save yourself?" This was just another form of "Physician, heal yourself."

Despite all this pain and much more, Jesus lived as the ultimate protector. It is written all over his life, but it comes into clarity while he is on the cross. He physically protected us by taking the punishment that we were due. He spiritually protected us by making a way for our salvation. While hanging in agony, he asked John to care for his mother—an act of relational and financial protection to ensure all her needs would be met when she was left alone.

Jesus had problems. Maybe not the same ones I have, but he understands me. He knows what it is like to be lonely, misunderstood, abandoned, confused, and in pain.

He proves that the best protectors aren't the people with perfect lives. The best protectors have bruises but push forward anyway. This is comforting because I am far from perfect. It also shines clarity on what I should expect from life—more bruises. Protectors willingly take them on so others don't have to.

God, it will be an honor to wear bruises earned by taking hits for others—be they physical, spiritual, relational, or financial. I am ready.

Prayer

Jesus, thank you for willingly taking bruises for me. You didn't run from pain or hardship but endured to the end to protect me. Even now, you don't run from my pain points but face them with me. You are so good. I want to emulate your protection today. Amen.

Get in the Game

1. Jesus died so we as protectors don't have to be perfect. Whatever guilt or shame you have hanging over your head needs to go. Read 1 John 1:9, then put it into action. Confess to God any sins that come to mind. Done? Then you are forgiven. Enter the remainder of your day free of guilt and shame, looking for the next opportunity to protect.

   OR

2. When we fail to protect, the best move is to own it, apologize, and do better in the future. Think back to a moment when you failed to adequately protect. Confess it to God and ask for another opportunity. If appropriate, apologize to any other parties involved and explain your desire to be a better protector in the future. You may get a bruise from that interaction, but wear it with pride. God is growing you.

WEEK
3

DAY 11

THE PATH OF PERSISTENCE
MEN HAVE A VISION

As for you, always be sober-minded, endure suffering, do the work of an evangelist, fulfill your ministry.

2 Timothy 4:5

Paul wrote these words to his protégé, Timothy, who was living on his own and caring for fledgling churches Paul had planted. It was a big vision for such a young man to fulfill.

The attitudes and actions Paul describes still carry weight today. They are the path to beginning, persisting in, and accomplishing any vision.

1. *Be sober-minded.* This means keeping a clear head. Emotional decisions are almost always the wrong decision. Take pride and expectation out of the equation, and make decisions that move the vision forward.

2. *Endure suffering.* The things separating you from your vision are time and difficulty. It's always been this way for any vision worth chasing. Expect it, and when it comes, you'll respond and press on instead of giving up.

3. *Do the work of an evangelist.* Evangelists draw people to them (and their message) because they're fun, light, and winsome. A curmudgeon with a big vision is still a curmudgeon. Laugh. Enjoy some time off with friends. Sleep. Bring a smile to your vision, not a scowl, and you'll draw other people to it.

4. *Fulfill your ministry.* Focus on the unique calling and mandate that God has given you. Fulfill YOUR ministry. Too much of our self-worth, or lack thereof, comes from comparing ourselves to others. That's always a losing game. You have your God-given vision and life, and I have mine. We are not in competition.

Every powerful man of vision is intimately acquainted with these four attributes. When others need a buzz, we embrace sobriety. When the boys complain about difficulty, we accept suffering as part of what comes with vision. When others want to be "discovered," we do the work of telling others about our vision and wooing them to be a part of it. When those who are unfocused hop from one thing to the next, we are focused on fulfilling the thing that God has put in front of us.

Paul and Timothy followed these four steps down the path of persistence and blessed untold millions in the process. If you belong to a church today, you are on the downline of their vision. These attributes worked then, and they are still the key to a powerful life of vision now.

Prayer

Lord, help me today to fulfill the things you put before me. I want to persist and not give up on the visions you have for my life. I commit myself to movement today. Amen.

Get in the Game

1. Reread today's verse, then answer two questions:
   (1) Which of Paul's four pieces of advice is the most
   difficult for you? (2) Who do you know that handles
   it well? Get time on their calendar and see what you
   can learn from their wisdom and experience.

   OR

2. Racehorses wear blinders to keep them focused on
   the task at hand. What is distracting you from fulfilling
   your ministry? Put on blinders today and get moving.
   That might mean shutting down social media, silenc-
   ing push notifications, or finding space to be alone.

DAY 12

BLESSED ARE . . .
MEN TAKE MINORITY POSITIONS

> Blessed are the poor in spirit, for theirs is the kingdom
> of heaven.
> Blessed are those who mourn, for they shall be
> comforted.
> Blessed are the meek, for they shall inherit the earth.
> Blessed are those who hunger and thirst for
> righteousness, for they shall be satisfied.
>
> Matthew 5:3–6

Jesus starts his most famous teaching, what we call the
Sermon on the Mount, with nine "Blessed are . . ." statements. They read like a manifesto for minority positions.
Each one would have been utterly shocking to the original
audience. If we can get past our familiarity with them, they
are just as shocking today.

When we read the word *blessed*, our mind jumps to
thoughts of God as a benevolent Santa Claus figure,

dipping his sugar finger into our life and making all our problems disappear. That's not what being blessed means.

In Greek, the original language of the New Testament, the word translated as "blessed" has multiple meanings, including "fortunate," "enlarged," and "favored." Our lives grow larger when we go through difficulty. And because God is near to the brokenhearted, what looks like a curse to the outside world is actually a blessing because it draws us nearer to God (see Ps. 34:18).

Jesus can say countercultural things like "blessed are the poor in spirit" and "blessed are those who mourn" because God is enlarging their lives. When we willingly step into these roles, we take a minority position that will result in our lives getting larger too.

We will be blessed if we do the things that other people aren't willing to do. In this section of Scripture, that would include:

- Hungering for righteousness instead of being a foodie
- Being content with an impoverished spirit instead of building up our reputation
- Willfully doing and believing things that will lead to persecution

- Being more excited about a reward in heaven than a pay raise

- Not expressing indignant anger and rage

- Not using our eyes as sexual portals that lead to lust

- Fulfilling our vow to our spouse

- Not retaliating but instead turning the other cheek

- Blessing people who have different political convictions instead of treating them like an enemy

The reason so few people feel blessed is because the vast majority of people are living the wrong way. It's not until we start to swim upstream, against the tide of culture, that our lives begin to grow larger. That is being blessed.

Prayer

God, I want to be blessed by you. I want to live a life that is growing larger, even if that means I look foolish to the rest of the world. You are worth far more than any minor discomfort I may receive for taking this minority position. I choose you today. Amen.

Get in the Game

1. Read Jesus's nine countercultural "blessed are" statements for yourself in Matthew 5:1–12. Now read them again but slower. Which "blessed are" statement sticks out the most to you today? Find a way to put it into practice. Whether it's spending time with someone who is mourning or choosing to have mercy when someone else has wronged you, know that your minority position is resulting in your life growth. You are actively being blessed.

   OR

2. Where does your life feel difficult? This could be the area where God is looking to bless or enlarge you. Take time to ask him to do that today, then be on the lookout for what he might be asking you to do. If you feel a nudge, jump into action.

DAY 13

A TEAM THAT WORKS
MEN ARE TEAM PLAYERS

Rebekah . . . came out with her water jar on her shoulder.
. . . She went down to the spring and filled her jar and came
up. Then the servant ran to meet her and said, "Please give
me a little water to drink from your jar." She said, "Drink, my
lord." And she quickly let down her jar upon her hand and
gave him a drink. When she had finished giving him a drink,
she said, "I will draw water for your camels also, until they
have finished drinking." So she quickly emptied her jar into
the trough and ran again to the well to draw water, and she
drew for all his camels.

Genesis 24:15–20

There might be no "I" in team, but there's no arguing that
great players elevate everyone else around them. Jordan
changed the Bulls. Brady took the Patriots over the top.
Any soccer team that adds Messi automatically becomes a
contender.

It's the same with the most important team in your life: marriage. The spouse you choose will either double the impact of your life or cut it in half.

In Genesis, God begins building a nation that will be his conduit of blessing to the rest of humanity. He promises an elderly couple they will have a son who will be the beginning of this dynasty. That's Isaac. When it's time for Isaac to find a wife, his father, Abraham, sends out a servant to look for the right woman.

There's a lot riding on this choice. If God's nation is going to last more than one generation, Isaac needs to have multiple healthy children—and not just physically healthy but spiritually healthy.

One of the markers of a spiritually healthy person is having a high work ethic when it comes to serving others. Abraham's servant understands this, so he sets up a little test as he reaches his destination and stops by the local well one evening. When all the women from town come to draw water, he will ask them for a drink. The one who volunteers to also water his camels (without being asked) will be the one for his master's son. He prays to God, asking for his blessing. That's when Rebekah enters the scene.

A quick Google search tells me that a typical camel can drink fifty-three gallons of water in three minutes.[1] Earlier in

Genesis 24, we're told that Abraham's servant was accompanied by ten camels (v. 10). You can do the math, but it's clear: Rebekah is working her noogies off. Carrying a heavy stone jar full of water, she makes multiple trips back and forth to the well to draw enough for the entire camel train to be satisfied.

Abraham's servant is blown away and wastes no time getting to the business of marriage. Someone who has that degree of hustle is going to make a great wife for Isaac and a great matriarch for the nation of Israel.

The best marriages don't happen because two soulmates find each other. They happen because two people have great work ethics in serving one another. A fifty-fifty marriage isn't good enough. Even if your spouse isn't giving 100 percent, that is not permission for you to slack off. I must willfully and creatively serve my wife—and not just when I'm asked. Like Rebekah, I need to notice what needs to be done and then complete it. She saw that the camels needed water and went to work without Abraham's servant saying a word.

Marriage is the greatest team you will ever be part of, and it will go to the next level if your goal is working hard to serve your wife. Whether you are married or not, you can find a way to serve someone else today. In doing that, you will be following in the footsteps of Jesus, who came "not to be served but to serve" (Matt. 20:28).

That's the type of work ethic that changes things.

Prayer

Father, I have a lot to learn from the example of Rebekah. I want to work hard to serve others and to serve you. When I see a problem, I want to take the initiative to fix it. I will work hard to be a blessing to someone else today. In doing that, I trust I am also blessing you. Amen.

Get in the Game

1. If you are married, go out of your way to serve your wife today. Whether it's finally fixing that leaky faucet she's been asking about, treating her to dinner at her favorite restaurant, or booking the vacation, do something that feels like a blessing to her. If you aren't married, find a way to bless someone else, no strings attached.

   OR

2. Think about the teams that you are on (marriage, work, friendships, etc.). Are you a team player who multiplies that team's effectiveness, or do you cut it in half? What recent evidence do you have to back up your answer? If you don't like your honest assessment, focus on serving that team today. It could be the first step to changing that team's culture.

DAY 14

THE WORK WE CAN'T DO
MEN WORK

> Whatever your hand finds to do, do it with your might, for there is no work or thought or knowledge or wisdom in Sheol, to which you are going.
>
> Ecclesiastes 9:10

As a young pastor, I was asked to perform multiple weddings every year. Celebrating the new unified life of a couple was an exciting event, as were the food, drinks, and dancing afterward. As I've gotten older, however, I've come to actually appreciate funerals even more. While it sounds morbid, it really isn't. For me, funerals bring a degree of clarity to life we find nowhere else except for Scriptures like this.

In the Old Testament, *Sheol* is a general name given to the place where everyone goes after death. It isn't a reward like heaven or a punishment like hell but just a separation from the land of the living.

The ancients have us beat on this one. In the Western world, we do everything we can to ignore, minimize, and dismiss death. What's the first thing we do when we hear someone has died? Ask how it happened. We're looking for any reason why the same fate won't catch up to us. If the recently deceased smoked or rode motorcycles or worked a dangerous job, we're somehow comforted.

The reality is that the death rate is still hovering at 100 percent. Today could be the day someone crosses the double yellow lines and takes me out on the way to work. Today could be the day a lump forms on my body, bringing with it bad news. Today could be the day an accident in my garage causes an injury I can't recover from.

I know people who can't physically speak what I just wrote. They fear that even voicing something bad that could happen to them might lead to it actually happening. They might remain silent, but it doesn't make this fact any less true.

I find that, rather than being depressing, this perspective invigorates me to use today well. There is some work I can do today that I won't be able to do in heaven. This life is the only time I can comfort a hurting friend. It is the only time I can coach my kids in their spiritual development. It is the only time I can introduce someone to Jesus for the first time, feed the poor, start a nonprofit, or pray for my neighbor.

I can get caught up in the rat race of the daily grind just like anyone else, but verses like this one remind me that today is a gift. No amount of seat belts, helmets, medical check-ups, or insurance policies can fully avert disaster. My life is more limited than I care to admit.

I can't control when my life vanishes, but I can control how I live my life. Today, I choose joy, obedience, and an aggressive stance. I choose to put in the hard work for the things that matter most—the things that can't be done on the other side.

If today is my last day, I am determined to make it count.

Prayer

Lord, this is a splash of cold water I find invigorating. I reject the fear of death and the fantasy of a never-ending life here on earth. I choose to live today boldly, with an eye toward your purposes and plans. I am looking for the opportunities you send my way and I am willing to work at them. Amen.

Get in the Game

1. If you knew you were going to die today, what would be your biggest regret? Go and do something about that today. Don't put it off any longer.

   OR

2. Hospice nurses report that relationships are the biggest source of either sorrow or joy when someone is facing death. How are your closest relationships? No matter your answer, choose a relationship and make a deposit today. You might take a walk with your spouse and talk, shoot hoops with your son, call your best friend to catch up, or check in on your parents. Relationships are always worth the work.

DAY 15

SHARPEN THE BLADE
MEN ARE PROTECTORS

> If the iron is blunt, and one does not sharpen the edge,
>> he must use more strength,
>> but wisdom helps one to succeed.
>>
>>> Ecclesiastes 10:10

Self-help gurus have made a lot of money off this verse. Stephen Covey taught us to "sharpen the saw," and others have used a similar idea of "sharpening the axe." Solomon, the wisest man in the world, was the first to give us this metaphor.

Personal growth and personal maintenance are critically intertwined. I can't just do the right things. In order to be effective and not get worn out, I have to be in the right shape and condition as I do the right things.

We recently had a training at work around responding to an active aggressor. While fighting back is one of the last resorts, there is the possibility it could come to that. In that event, we were trained to look for weapons in everyday items—things we could hold on to and use repeatedly to bring bodily harm to an active shooter. Things like chairs or fire extinguishers could work, as well as objects with sharp points like scissors, blades, or sharpened pencils.

I hope I never have to use that training, but it reinforced the biblical wisdom of this passage: you are a better protector when you are sharp.

Personally, I hate taking the time to sharpen kitchen utensils, my chain saw chain, and my hunting knives. It always feels like there is something more pressing that would be a better use of my time. But failing to do this easy maintenance means that when I need them most, my blades won't be ready to perform. A dull cutting edge means harder, less effective, and less enjoyable work.

Similarly, I can always find reasons not to do the things that sharpen me—things like practicing a weekly day of rest (called a Sabbath in the Bible), regular date nights with my wife, workouts at my local gym, or making space for fun with friends. Reading the Bible and prayer are disciplines that will be dropped if I see them as a duty instead of a personal blessing. Each of these is an opportunity to be sharpened so that I will be a more effective protector when the time comes.

Maybe the biggest factor to sharpness, though, is the thing most of us try to put off every night: sleep. Rest isn't just physical, it is spiritual. When we don't sleep well, we are inviting physical problems into our life and making it harder to run on all cylinders spiritually. I am convinced nothing influences whether or not I have a good day as much as whether or not I slept well the night before.

I'm not ashamed to say I got nine hours last night. I heard a doctor recently say that we have a statistically greater chance of winning multiple gold medals at the Olympics than being one of the rare people who need less than eight hours of sleep. Sleep is a daily sharpening given to us from God (Ps. 127:2). We need to stop leaving the gift on the table unopened.

Putting off sharpening may work for a day, but in the long run you are inviting trouble and burnout to find you. It is a good thing to devote time, resources, and intention to making ourselves sharp and fit tools in the hands of God.

The people you protect are depending on you to have a cutting edge. Don't put off the sharpening.

Prayer

God, I find the temptation to avoid sharpening is persistent. I don't want to be a dull tool in your hands. Put opportunities for me to be sharpened in my field of vision today and I will take them. Amen.

Get in the Game

1. Where in your life are you feeling dull? Make time today to do something that will sharpen that aspect of your life. If your marriage is listless, take your wife on a date she'd enjoy. If your physical health is stalled out, try a new workout routine. If your spiritual life needs a boost, push yourself to spend thirty minutes alone with God. If your financial life is dull, seek out wisdom from an expert or friend who is good with money. Whatever you do, do something. Sharpening doesn't happen by accident.

    OR

2. Whatever it takes, commit to getting at least eight hours of sleep tonight, then take notice of your mood, work ethic, and effectiveness tomorrow. Getting adequate sleep is a simple and challenging choice that will leave you sharper.

WEEK
4

DAY 16

A RISING TIDE
MEN HAVE A VISION

> They devoted themselves to the apostles' teaching and
> the fellowship, to the breaking of bread and the prayers.
> And awe came upon every soul, and many wonders and
> signs were being done through the apostles. And all who
> believed were together and had all things in common. And
> they were selling their possessions and belongings and
> distributing the proceeds to all, as any had need. . . . And
> the Lord added to their number day by day those who were
> being saved.
>
> Acts 2:42–45, 47

The book of Acts is always refreshing to me. It is the story
of the early church banding together and going on an
adventure.

The first believers played by different rules, and as a result,
they operated with a different power. Jesus gave them a vision to not be about themselves and to aggressively spread

the good news to others in near and far-off places. They took him at his word and went for it.

If the original disciples had a conversation with a modern American believer, they wouldn't recognize our spirituality. They had a vision to be outward-focused; we have tunnel vision on ourselves. They were focused on bringing more people into the fold; we ask what the church can do for us. They developed deep communal connections; we elevate rugged individualism. They sacrificed to bless outsiders; we fight to get votes for our preferred party. Their vision was on growing the eternal kingdom of God; we fixate on the temporal state of America, our bank account, or our favorite sports team. They turned to prayer first; we turn to Google, self-help mantras, medication, and rationalization. Maybe, when we run out of options, we will remember to pray.

Is it any wonder we're so anemic? These words from Acts are a far cry from describing the modern church experience in America. But they don't have to be.

I don't want to go back to the first century. I like indoor plumbing, grilling steaks, and riding my motorcycle. The first church had their own set of problems. But something they had that we often lack was a commitment to a vision larger than their own individual improvement. They modeled what we should still be doing.

Open the aperture and take a wider look. Where is your vision too narrow, and how can you consider others more important than yourself (see Phil. 2:3)?

A rising tide lifts all boats.

Prayer

God, the story of Acts is a hard reset for what life could and should be like. I want to be more dependent upon you, more ingrained in community, and more driven by the vision of Jesus to bless others. Give me a chance to do that today and I will jump on it. Amen.

Get in the Game

1. Having vision isn't an excuse to be selfish. In the spirit of the early church, keep your eyes open today for someone you can bless. When you first feel the prompting, jump on it. It might be as simple as buying a coffee for a stranger or as complex as opening your home to someone in need. Choose your own adventure.

   OR

2. Prayer was one of the primary tools the early believers utilized. When was the last time you prayed about your vision? Spend time today doing just that. Get into the specifics with God, make asks, and expect answers.

DAY 17

LEAVING SHAME BEHIND
MEN TAKE MINORITY POSITIONS

> And you, who were dead in your trespasses . . . God made
> alive together with him, having forgiven us all our trespasses,
> by canceling the record of debt that stood against us with
> its legal demands. This he set aside, nailing it to the cross.
>
> Colossians 2:13–14

Shame will stop you from moving. It will stunt your growth,
keeping your eyes focused on mistakes of the past rather
than new things God is doing around you.

Mistakes are like motorcycle wrecks, of which I've had a
few. Once you get your wits about you, you have to climb
back on the bike and conquer the fear that wants to walk
the rest of the way instead. If you don't, you will never ride
again.

Shame is an awful and oppressive thing because it does
that. Not the conviction of sin, which so many people try to
ignore, but rather the residual guilt that exists in our minds

even though it doesn't exist in God's mind any longer. If you have cleared the air with God and chosen to walk a new direction, then you are good.

In ancient times, once someone was out of financial debt, the person who loaned the money and held the note would publicly nail it to a board in the town square for all to see. This was a proclamation that the debt had been paid in full and the person was released from all obligations. When Jesus is nailed to a cross, it is God's public declaration that we are free and forgiven.

Taking minority positions is hard. If it wasn't, boys would do it and it wouldn't be one of the marks of a man. When I look back into my past, I can think of multiple times I wish I had a do-over—times when I missed a minority position or just ignored it outright because of fear or convenience or pressure from others. There may be a lesson to learn from those failures, but if I sit in that shame, I will miss the next opportunity that comes my way.

Feeling shame over something Jesus has already forgiven me for devalues the steep price he paid on the cross. Our graceless culture might cancel me at any time, but the only canceling my heavenly Father does is of my sin.

That kind of freedom not only clears my past, it clears my vision for the day ahead.

Prayer

Father, I am sorry for the minority positions I have failed to take in the past. I want to do better. Now that I have apologized, I choose to believe in the freedom Jesus won for me. I am leaving shame behind, so I am ready to move on the next minority position you put in front of me. Amen.

Get in the Game

1. When you think of missed opportunities to take a minority position in your past, what comes to mind? Choose one. Apologize to God for that specific situation, and if it involves someone else, apologize to them as well. Once you've done that, you are free. Leave it behind and move into freedom.

   OR

2. Where in your life are shame and fear keeping you locked up? Today is the day to get back up on the bike. Commit to doing one thing today to move your life beyond the shame of your past. I am convinced the more steps you take, the more freedom you will feel. That begins right now.

DAY 18

WALKING OUT OF THE ORPHANAGE
MEN ARE TEAM PLAYERS

> Even before he made the world, God loved us and chose
> us in Christ to be holy and without fault in his eyes. God
> decided in advance to adopt us into his own family by
> bringing us to himself through Jesus Christ. This is what he
> wanted to do, and it gave him great pleasure.
>
> Ephesians 1:4–5 NLT

Everyone who knows God came to him the same way:
adoption.

This means that everyone is born a spiritual orphan. We remain that way until we receive Jesus, accepting the adoption he won for us through his death and resurrection.

The orphan mindset—fighting for resources, attention,
and love—explains so much about our current culture. We
are terrible to each other because another orphan in the

orphanage means less to go around. We feel threatened. We compete. We pull others down to make us feel better about ourselves. When we scroll past someone doing better than us, we lose our bearings and fall into jealousy.

The orphanage is a terrible place to live, and as long as it's your primary residence, you'll have a hard time belonging to a team.

As a child of adoption, I naturally move toward orphan thinking. Even now, having followed Christ for decades, I still have to actively fight the orphan inside. I do that by reminding myself of the truths that Scripture speaks about me:

1. I am a child of God who is fully loved by my heavenly Father (John 3:16).

2. God will never leave me or forsake me (Deut. 31:8).

3. It doesn't matter what someone else has (or doesn't have), God has plans and a purpose for me (Jer. 29:11).

4. God chose me for his family, and it gives him great pleasure (Eph. 1:4–6).

Last year, I got to spend a week with other pastors at a sweet hunting lodge in Florida. It sits on a bunch of property and is owned by a local church. When I first arrived, my orphan heart wanted to play the comparison game: *How can this church afford this when they are smaller than the church I lead?* Then, while spending time with other pastors, I caught myself looking for cues in their stories (and attendance numbers and giving totals and strategic hires) to tell me if I was doing a good job or not.

My orphan heart nearly sucked the joy out of the whole experience. Thankfully, I caught it in time. I apologized to God for playing the comparison game and spent the rest of the event looking to encourage others instead of jockeying for points.

In the book of Romans, Paul tells the church members there to "rejoice with those who rejoice, weep with those who weep. Live in harmony with one another" (Rom. 12:15–16).

When you celebrate the wins of someone else even when you are losing, you're being a team player. When you can mourn with someone hurting even when things are going great for you, you're being a team player. When you can put away comparison to live in harmony, you're being a team player.

Christ adopted us and broke open the doors of the orphanage. It's high time we walked out . . . together.

Prayer

God, I am sorry that orphan thinking still has such a grip on me. Today, I choose to reject comparison. I trust what you are doing in me, and I choose to celebrate the good things you are doing in others. I want to leave the orphanage behind. Amen.

Get in the Game

1. Where do you feel the pull of orphan thinking, and how is it influencing your ability to be a team player? Which of the four Scripture truths listed earlier do you need to focus on to combat that? Work on committing that verse to memory today.

    OR

2. Take Paul's advice from Romans 12 to heart. Who do you know that is rejoicing and on top of the world? Reach out to them with some encouragement today and celebrate the good going on in their life. Who do you know that is weeping and feeling hurt? Call to check in on them and lend your support. By focusing on the good of others, you're robbing comparison of its power. Well done.

DAY 19

IN THE TENSION
MEN WORK

A man wrestled with [Jacob] until the breaking of the day. When the man saw that he did not prevail against Jacob, he touched his hip socket, and Jacob's hip was put out of joint as he wrestled with him. Then he said, "Let me go, for the day has broken." But Jacob said, "I will not let you go unless you bless me." . . . Then [the man] said, "Your name shall no longer be called Jacob, but Israel, for you have striven with God and with men, and have prevailed."

Genesis 32:24–26, 28

Jacob gets a bad rap from many traditional Bible teachers. Mostly because many Bible teachers are passive people who study but don't do. Jacob is a doer. He is a worker. He is a hustler. He is a fighter. He has his faults, but none of those attributes are among them because those attributes aren't faults.

Scholars believe the "man" wrestling with Jacob was anything from an angel to a preincarnate Jesus. Because of the blessing Jacob gets at the end, I am prone to believe it was God.

When a man wrestles God, it really isn't a contest. God is toying with Jacob like a dad toys with his toddler while "wrestling" on the floor. Even though God has to only slightly tap Jacob's hip to dislocate it, the pain would have been excruciating for Jacob. Despite this pain, Jacob works and fights just to hang on. Why? He realizes he has hold of someone with greater power and authority than his own, and he wants to be blessed.

Maybe the reason more of us don't receive blessings is that we aren't willing to work, hustle, or barely hold on for a little while longer. These are attributes that God admires—so much so that he gives Jacob a new name: God's fighter (Israel).

Like his grandfather, Abraham, and his father, Isaac, Jacob finds success in life because of the grace of God *and* his hard work. It is a powerful combo when we take, develop, and deploy our natural abilities while at the same time living in a way that invites the blessings of God into our lives.

This is why I look at Jacob as a spiritual hero. It is why I named my son Jacob. And it is why our family motto has always been "Tomes hustle." I have made many mistakes and I will make more, but passivity will not be one of them. I want to place myself in the stream of God's blessing, and I want to work hard in the process.

No question, there are things that God is going to bring my way, out of his grace, that I don't have to work for. Equally, it's no question that there are blessings that will only come my way if I'm willing to work. Jacob is a great example of living in this tension.

Most of us get this wrong. Either we live with undue stress, anxiety, and constant worry because we don't recognize the X factor of God in our lives, thinking everything depends upon our own efforts, or we lack drive, ambition, and work ethic, content to wait for God to come by and dip his sugar finger into our lives.

This is not the way of God. It's not the way of Jacob. And it's not the way I will live.

The most potent lives are found in the tension of God's blessing and hard work.

Prayer

God, I will cling tightly to you today because I want your blessing. I don't control your movement in my life, but passivity will not be the reason my life stalls. I am honored to work hard for you today, and I am honored when you do things through me that I could never produce on my own. I am yours. Amen.

Get in the Game

1. Adopt my family motto for the day. Every time you get a chance, hustle—around the house, in the parking lot, at work, and beyond. The goal isn't to hurry but to move with purpose, clarity, and intention. Pay attention to what things break your way because of your willingness to move.

   OR

2. Live today in the tension of God's blessing and hard work. Start by asking God for a specific blessing. When you're finished, go ahead and start moving on it, even if God hasn't answered yet. Asking for financial blessing? Call the bank and set up a savings account. Want to get married? Introduce yourself to someone today. Need a breakthrough at work? Schedule the overdue meeting with your manager. Learn to live in the tension, and look for God to move.

DAY 20

SIGHTS ON THE ENEMY
MEN ARE PROTECTORS

Finally, be strong in the Lord and in the strength of his might. Put on the whole armor of God, that you may be able to stand against the schemes of the devil. For we do not wrestle against flesh and blood, but against the rulers, against the authorities, against the cosmic powers over this present darkness, against the spiritual forces of evil in heavenly places.

Ephesians 6:10–12

Why are we so surprised when life gets hard? We shouldn't be. We live in a war zone where there is an enemy who marshals cosmic forces to knock us down and off our spiritual game. His name is Satan, and he is aided by demons who inflict pain and confusion in personal and powerful ways.

This isn't a fact to be feared but acknowledged. Interestingly, our lack of acknowledgment might be Satan's greatest tool.

A recent Gallup poll of Americans found that belief in God and the devil have hit all-time lows: 74 percent of Americans believe in God, while only 58 percent believe in the devil.[1] That disparity between the two statistics suggests there are plenty of people who believe in God but not his cosmic enemy. That is to our detriment because a hidden enemy is one with the upper hand.

I recently hosted both a former spy for the CIA and a legitimate, trained-in-Rome exorcist on my podcast. Each conversation taught me about my enemy.

Embedded in the Middle East, the spy was most effective at her job when she remained hidden. She would shop at different stores each week, drive different routes to work, even leave her home at different times each day to avoid detection. She operated in the shadows. Satan is happy to do the same.

The exorcist, despite what you might expect from the movies, was a man full of light. He was joyful, funny, and a pleasure to spend an hour with. He was so open to sharing his remarkable life and stories because the more light he shines on the enemy, the less effective that enemy becomes.

We can't see Satan or his demons with our eyeballs. But we should be able to recognize the systems he has set up to thwart the will of God and crush our souls. Systems of workaholism that keep us slaving away on the hamster wheel while we get nowhere. Systems of judgmentalism that cause us to constantly compare ourselves to others and feel like a "loser" or "winner" with every judgmental interaction. Systems of injustice that cause some people to have a harder time than others as a result of their DNA. Just because we can't see the machinery doesn't mean that the outputs aren't real.

I did a bunch of elk hunting this past year and didn't see a single elk, but I know they were there—I saw their tracks and droppings everywhere. It's the same with Satan. I see his tracks and droppings in stats around mental health, suicide, and loneliness. I see them in the destruction of divorces and bankruptcy. I see them when believers walk away from the faith. I can see his work of angst and disharmony in the perpetual tension and judgmentalism between different people groups.

Today's Scripture passage names our enemy. It isn't the other political party, our disrespectful neighbor, an antagonist at work, or a destructive family member. We are squared off against spiritual forces of evil. The more they can keep us fighting each other, the less focused we will be on them.

It is true that not every bad thing that happens in life has a spiritual root. We all make choices, and when we make bad ones, we live with the consequences. But the truth remains that we are in a spiritual war and should expect spiritual shrapnel.

In order to stand against the enemy, we need the armor and weapons detailed in Ephesians 6. But we will never get dressed for battle until we believe there is an enemy to fight.

Prayer

God, I believe that you are more powerful than Satan. I am not afraid of him, but I do acknowledge that he wants to knock me off my game. Thank you for giving me spiritual armor to fight back. I declare war on your enemies today. Amen.

Get in the Game

1. Get outfitted for the battle ahead. Read Ephesians
   6:10–20. Which pieces of armor or weapons do you
   need most today? Ask God to equip you, then go
   about your day believing that he has. You are ready.

   OR

2. The enemy you know has less power over you than
   the one lurking in the shadows. Shine a light on
   God's enemy by listening to my podcast conversation
   with exorcist Father Vincent Lampert titled "Standing
   Up to the Devil." Search for *The Aggressive Life with
   Brian Tome* podcast in Google or wherever you listen
   to podcasts.

WEEK
5

DAY 21

RIGOR AND VIGOR
MEN HAVE A VISION

> And they brought to him a man who was deaf and had a speech impediment, and they begged him to lay his hand on him. And taking him aside from the crowd privately, he put his fingers into his ears, and after spitting touched his tongue. . . . And his ears were opened, his tongue was released, and he spoke plainly.
>
> Mark 7:32–33, 35

Mark records the inside scoop the rest of the gathering crowd doesn't get to see: the theatrics of Jesus's prayer leading to healing. They're done privately and not in front of a studio audience for publicity.

Jesus does what he does in order to get results, and he's willing to look weird to do it.

When Jesus prays it is often punctuated with the physical, the tactile, and even the bizarre. Sticking fingers into someone else's ears is odd. Spitting on your fingers and then touching someone else's tongue will earn you a citation from the CDC. I'm convinced we don't see more miracles in prayer for two reasons illustrated by this story.

1. *Initiative.* By my count, Jesus performs forty-one miracles in the Bible. Of those, thirty-four involve the sick person (or a close friend) directly asking Jesus for help. Of the remaining seven, at least five involve the healed person having to do something to show their faith in Jesus's power (e.g., reaching out, stepping forward, washing in a pool). When you passively wait for something good to happen, all you reap is boredom.

2. *Full engagement.* Prayer isn't just silence with our heads bowed. Those of us who think or act like that's all it is have anemic prayer lives. Instead, prayer thrives with rigor and vigor. It is an act of faith that comes through the movement of our body, not just checking a mental box. Do we not creatively engage prayer because we don't believe it? Because we don't want to be embarrassed? Or because we ignore the example of Jesus? He touches the diseased (Matt. 8:3), casts out demons with a strong voice (Matt. 8:32), and prays hard enough to bleed (Luke 22:44). If you can walk and chew gum at the same time, maybe try walking around your neighborhood

and praying. Any way you can bring your full engagement to prayer will take it to the next level.

Prayer isn't passive or a last resort. It is an act of faith that changes things in the spiritual realm. Sometimes those changes are manifested in the physical realm as well. We call those miracles.

Push all your chips in on prayer. Come at it with rigor and vigor. Take initiative, bring your full engagement, and be willing to look weird.

To experience something different we have to do something different.

Prayer

God, I do not think of you as passive or weak, so my prayers to you shouldn't be either. I want to see your power at work in my life, and I am willing to do what it takes to see that happen. Amen.

Get in the Game

1. Take initiative in your prayers today. Ask God to provide a major breakthrough in your vision or to perform a specific miracle. No matter his answer, I believe he will be pleased with your boldness to ask because asking demonstrates faith.

   OR

2. Engage prayer differently today. We can all get into a rut when we repeat the same patterns day after day, so try something new. You might kneel on the ground, go for a walk, pray inside a quiet chapel, or ask someone you admire to pray over you with their hands on your shoulders. Push through the discomfort and see what God does.

DAY 22

THE PRIMARY FILTER
MEN TAKE MINORITY POSITIONS

> Our God whom we serve is able to deliver us from the
> burning fiery furnace, and he will deliver us out of your
> hand, O king. But if not, be it known to you, O king, that we
> will not serve your gods or worship the golden image that
> you have set up.
>
> Daniel 3:17–18

In the ancient world, to know someone's name was to
know something about them. Their name was their identity.
You may have heard the names Shadrach, Meshach, and
Abednego, but that's not who they were. It wasn't their true
identity.

Their parents had named them Hananiah, Mishael, and
Azariah. These young men were living in Israel when it was
conquered by the Babylonians. They were taken away from
their homeland and forced to live in exile. Recognized as
some of the brightest and best among the Jews, they were
singled out for training in the Babylonian culture in order

to serve the king. But their training was more like brain-washing. Among other things, each one was given a new Babylonian name, a forced identity meant to root out their devotion to their God.

The name Hananiah means "God is gracious." The Babylonians changed his name to Shadrach, which means "command of Aku," one of the Babylonian gods. The name Mishael means "who is like our God?" His name was changed to Meshach, which means "who is what Aku is?" The name Azariah means "God has helped." He was re-named Abednego, which means "servant of Nebo," a reference to another Babylonian god.

When the Babylonian king builds a golden statue of himself and expects everyone in the land to worship it or face certain death in a fiery furnace, the men who stand before him and refuse aren't acting like the Babylonian identities they have been given. It is Hananiah, Mishael, and Azariah who turn down the king.

In their speech, they say that God is *able* to deliver them, not that God *will* deliver them. They know it isn't guaranteed or even likely that a miracle will take place. That doesn't matter to them. As servants of the true God, they will not bend their knee to any idol, no matter the consequence. Pleasing God is their top motivator. Everything else is second.

Taking minority positions gets much simpler when pleasing God is my primary filter. These three men knew flames were in their future, but they believed the pain of that would only be temporary. The pain of capitulating and taking the easy road would have lasted much, much longer.

Whether God would deliver them or not (spoiler alert: he did), they were determined to be faithful and do the right thing, no matter the consequence. It was actually in the furnace where they met God. It was in the flames where they experienced their names being lived out—they found that God was a helper, gracious, and unlike any other god in the land.

There isn't another you. When you fully embrace your God-given identity, you will always find yourself in the minority. This is a profound truth and motivation to move today.

Prayer

God, I am inspired by the faith of your three servants. Even under the constant pressure of Babylon, pleasing you was their primary motivator. Give me their vision today and their boldness to step into flames when I need to. Whether you deliver me or not, I will be faithful. Amen.

Get in the Game

1. Take stock of your life. Where does it feel like you are in the flames? Ask God to meet you there. Whether he turns down the heat or not, trust that he is with you and is using it to form you.

   OR

2. From this moment until you go to bed tonight, choose "pleasing God" as your primary filter for the day. Let it inform and dictate the choices you make, the words you speak, and the minority positions you are willing to step into.

DAY 23

WELL SPENT
MEN ARE TEAM PLAYERS

> When Jesus saw his mother and the disciple whom he loved standing nearby, he said to his mother, "Woman, behold, your son!" Then he said to the disciple, "Behold, your mother!" And from that hour the disciple took her to his own home.
>
> John 19:26–27

There is not much to laugh about when it comes to the crucifixion of Jesus, but this moment always makes me smile.

Throughout the Gospel he wrote, John refers to himself as "the disciple whom Jesus loved" (13:23; 19:26; 20:2; 21:7; 21:20). He gives this title to himself and shares it with no one else. He is a close friend of Jesus and is definitely loved. But his best friend? Seems like a stretch. Still, when I read about the life of Jesus and see his patterns around male friendship, there's something for me to learn.

Most men don't have friends. We have associates we work with. We might have memories of friends from college, but we aren't actively engaged in their lives anymore. The biggest epidemic our world has ever faced is loneliness. We are still squarely in the midst of it. This is part of the reason why men have a life expectancy five years less than women,[1] die by suicide at four times the rate of women,[2] and are two times more likely to have an alcohol-related incident or death.[3]

Many men call someone their best friend because they only have one friend—and usually that relationship isn't very deep. The men I know who have healthy relational lives don't have a best friend. Instead, they have a handful of friends they consider top-tier. Jesus had twelve close friends, and among them his top-tier were Peter, James, and John.

It cracks me up that John tried to immortalize himself as *the* best friend, even though Jesus never called him that. (John also went to great lengths to let us all know he was faster than Peter. Equally as hilarious. Find that in John 20:3–4.) Instead, Jesus leaned into different friends in different ways at different times.

John was top-tier relationally, so Jesus asked him to take care of his mother, Mary. Peter was a top-tier aggressive leader, so Jesus placed him in charge of his movement, the church (Matt. 16:18; John 21:15–17). James had top-tier commitment and would become the first disciple to be killed for his faith (Acts 12:1–2).

Jesus established his top tier by investing extra into them. He often pulled these three aside to get time, teaching, and experiences the other nine disciples didn't receive (Matt. 17:1 and 26:37 are two examples).

Likewise, I need to continue to free up resources to grow and enjoy my top-tier friendships. In school, proximity helped you establish friends. Now you have to spend your money, time, and talents.

Resources spent on friends are resources well spent. When you develop your top tier, you're making a wise investment that will pay off for years to come.

Prayer

Jesus, your pattern for friendships works. I want to emulate that today. Give me vision about who needs to be in my top tier and how I can invest in them today. I do this to follow your example and to push back against loneliness. You are worth it all. Amen.

Get in the Game

1. Take stock of your friendships and ask God who needs to be in your top tier. Open a note in your phone and write down any names that come to mind. Then consider how you can invest something into each of them this week and write it out beside their name. Now go and get to building your team.

   OR

2. We can laugh at John's nickname for himself, but he was a man firmly rooted in his identity. Spend some time asking God what nickname he would give you. Remember, it will always be something that calls good out of you—something like "the one who works hard," "the one who doesn't give up," "the one who moves," or "the one who thinks of others." If a thought enters your mind, assume it's from God. How can you live more into that identity today?

DAY 24

QUIET, SIMPLE WORK
MEN WORK

> But we urge you, brothers, . . . to aspire to live quietly, and
> to mind your own affairs, and to work with your hands, as
> we instructed you.
>
> 1 Thessalonians 4:10–11

Here are three things that you will never see on anyone's
bucket list: living quietly, minding your own business, and
working with your hands. Paul not only sets these up as
ideals, he urges the church to live this way.

In contrast, nowadays our greatest ideals are the rights to
go viral, comment on the lives of others, and outsource as
much work as we can. It's no wonder our lives have mostly
gone shallow and weak.

For all of anthropological history, men have used their
hands to hunt, to build, to fix, to defend. Very few of us do
any of those things anymore. We get caught in the cultural
web of making a splash and hitting it big. We cultivate our

online presence, follow the right influencers, make the "approved" cultural choices—all the while dying on the inside.

All of this weighs heavily on the mental health of men in our world. I believe it is a major contributor to the reason we die earlier, die more often by suicide, and are more prone to abuse substances than women. We've lost the example of the greats who have gone before us—the men who worked hard, ran in their lane, and lived quietly.

In the book of Exodus, when God is giving directions for the building of his tabernacle where the Jews would go to worship him, he gives special encouragement and blessing to the tradesmen (35:35). Our culture geeks out on spiritual gifts like prophecy and speaking in tongues, and in the process we forget that our lives can't progress without the builders. Greater honor needs to go to the men who work with their hands, who build things, plumb things, wire things, paint things, and fix things. Working with our hands is something we can learn, but for some it is a supernatural gift from God.

I recently considered hiring someone to mow my lawn. It would have simplified my life, but this verse seals the deal: I won't be making that call. After a workday spent in strategy meetings and mentally preparing myself to speak, I need the discipline of working with my hands. Without it, I fear I would lose something that is good for my spiritual, mental, and physical health. Gassing, maintaining, and servicing a mower are critical skills—as is the mowing itself. When I put the power tools away and look at a completed yard, I get a sense of satisfaction that I never get from a Google document or email. The fact that no one will praise me for this yard work makes it even better. It is one way that I can live quietly, mind my own affairs, and work hard.

Very frequently it is the simple things in life that are closest to the heart of God—like quiet, simple work.

Prayer

Lord, your wisdom is countercultural, and it works. Today I want to live by this verse. Give me ideas on how I can live quietly, mind my own affairs, and work hard with my hands. Whatever you prompt me to do, I am in. Amen.

Get in the Game

1. Which of Paul's three pieces of advice jumps out to you the most? Find a way to put it into action today. Here are some ideas to get your wheels turning:

   - *Live quietly*—purposefully choose to be the last person to speak in meetings; ask others for their opinions; listen before you speak; spend time outside with no music or screens

   - *Mind your own affairs*—go twenty-four hours without any social media; unplug from the news; skip the sports game this weekend; spend quality time with family

   - *Work with your hands*—pick up litter everywhere you go; pull weeds for your elderly neighbor; start (or finish) the home project; volunteer to help a friend wrenching on their car

     OR

2. Read Exodus 35, looking for the emphasis God places on men who have the ability to work with their hands. If you are a blue-collar tradesman, go into work today knowing that God goes with you. If you are a white-collar worker, find a way to physically get your hands dirty today, trusting that God will meet you in the work you choose.

DAY 25

STRONG AND COURAGEOUS
MEN ARE PROTECTORS

All the spoil of these cities and the livestock, the people of
Israel took for their plunder. But every person they struck
with the edge of the sword until they had destroyed them,
and they did not leave any who breathed. Just as the LORD
had commanded Moses his servant, so Moses commanded
Joshua, and so Joshua did. He left nothing undone of all
that the LORD had commanded Moses.

Joshua 11:14–15

Many people have a problem with the violence in the Old
Testament of the Bible. They bristle at the fact that God's
people carried weapons, invaded territories, and put their
enemies to the sword. They struggle most with the fact that
these actions oftentimes were authorized by God. I don't.
These stories are a powerful reminder of a reality we are all
still living.

In this passage, God's people had been freed from genera-tions of slavery in Egypt and had finally made it to the land God promised to Abraham thousands of years earlier. God commissioned them to go and take it. Since the various tribes and people groups living in the land weren't just going to give it up, war ensued.

The people had to fight because passivity wouldn't take the promised land. It wouldn't open up new avenues to ex-perience God's blessing. It wouldn't protect what matters most.

It still works this way with me. Passive spirituality is a waste of time. I have to take the aggressive stance, strap on my sword, and conquer the things God is calling me to conquer. I face off against enemies that are trying to take ground in me—apathy, ruts in my marriage, disunity at work, orphaned thinking, selfishness—and I strike them down.

To be clear, God is never going to ask me to invade my neighbor's yard and kill him. These passages represent a unique period with God that hasn't been replicated since. Some scholars explain these violent passages by remind-ing us that these enemy groups would have killed God's people. Others point to the fact that some of these groups practiced pagan religions that included child sacrifice. God may have authorized this violence so that his people wouldn't be annihilated or tainted. Whether this is true or not, I've personally seen that people who struggle the most with the violence in the Bible often have a hard time strenuously taking new territory in their faith. They are slow to kill the things in themselves that don't please God.

The call to the nation of Israel and to us today is "be strong and courageous." These words come up again and again in the Bible. Moses spoke them as a command to Joshua just before the Israelites crossed the Jordan River into the promised land (Deut. 31:6). As Joshua took Moses's place as leader, God repeated them four times in one chapter (Josh. 1:6, 7, 9, 18). Joshua would later speak them to the entire nation of Israel as they worked to conquer the land before them (Josh. 10:25). Thousands of years later, they are some of the last words King David spoke over his son Solomon before his death (1 Chron. 28:20).

Strength and courage are needed as much now as they ever have been. God won't ask me to kill my enemy, but he may ask me to use my strength to bite my tongue and not return hurtful words in the heat of an argument. God won't ask me to invade another's land, but it will take courage for me to choose the path of humility and self-sacrifice. It takes strength to seek forgiveness when I've hurt someone, courage to live generously when money is tight, and both to kill the things inside me that don't please God.

The time period of biblical holy wars might be over, but God still calls his protectors to be strong and courageous. Spiritual war is the path to the promised land, and I will commit to putting to death anything inside me that stands in the way.

Prayer

God, I want to be strong and courageous. I will engage wherever you are calling me to go to battle today. Show me the parts of myself that need to be killed and I will act. Amen.

Get in the Game

1. Where in your life are you being lulled into passivity? Be strong and courageous today and take definitive action to push things forward. Whether it's initiating a hard conversation you have been putting off, pulling the trigger on a financial decision, taking ownership of a mistake and apologizing, or something else, move forward as an act of war against the enemy.

   OR

2. God's people didn't move into the promised land alone, and you shouldn't either. Invite a close and trusted brother into a battle you are facing. You might seek his advice, ask him to pray for you consistently, or just welcome his listening ear. There is strength in numbers.

WEEK
6

DAY 26

SOLDIER, ATHLETE, FARMER
MEN HAVE A VISION

> No soldier gets entangled in civilian pursuits, since his aim is to please the one who enlisted him. An athlete is not crowned unless he competes according to the rules. It is the hard-working farmer who ought to have the first share of the crops. Think over what I say, for the Lord will give you understanding in everything.
>
> 2 Timothy 2:4–7

Paul's letter to Timothy is full of actionable wisdom for the young missionary and church leader. Here, he uses three well-known occupations as illustrations for how Timothy is to live and operate with vision.

1. *Soldier.* There is only one vision for soldiers: to carry out the orders of their commanding officers. It is this sharp degree of clarity that allows them to act quickly in times of crisis and need. In order to do this, they

must put the distractions of civilian life behind them. A clouded mind brings confusion, distraction, and delay, both on and off the battlefield. Too many of us are entangled in civilian affairs instead of soldiering on.

2. *Athlete.* The world's greatest athletes train for years in order to have a chance to compete on their sport's biggest stage, be it the Super Bowl, the Olympics, or the World Cup. There is no guarantee their hard work will ever pay off, but their vision for what could be compels them to persist. When they do get the chance to compete, they do so according to the rules so their vision and training aren't wasted. You obey the rules so that you can actually win.

3. *Farmer.* Growing anything is incredibly difficult work. The farmers I have met work the longest hours and in the fiercest conditions of almost anyone else on this planet. They go after it, sunup to sundown, for a vision far in the distance. It is the small things they do every day that eventually bring a yield. That vision feeds an entire planet. We rely on them, and they truly deserve the first taste of the fruits of their labors. When we plant things that God wants planted and see those things through to fruition, we are the ones who benefit with the blessings and rewards of a job well done.

The soldier is focused. The athlete stays in his lane. The farmer faithfully does the little things to bring an increase. Our vision will go to the next level if we can follow their lead and do the same.

Prayer

God, you are good to use the seemingly mundane details of life to push us forward. There is something to be learned from the soldier, the athlete, and the farmer. Give me an idea of how I can emulate one of them today and I will do it. Amen.

Get in the Game

1. In the prayer above, you took Paul's advice and asked God to give you understanding. Now spend a few minutes thinking over each of these roles. Which one is the most resonant with you and your vision right now? How will you act on this learning today?

   OR

2. Take this learning one step deeper. Do you know a soldier, an athlete, or a farmer? Get some time on their calendar and ask them what they've learned from their own experiences about vision and how to implement it.

DAY 27

KEEP GOING
MEN TAKE MINORITY POSITIONS

> Ahab told Jezebel all that Elijah had done, and how he had killed all the prophets with the sword. Then Jezebel sent a messenger to Elijah, saying, "So may the gods do to me and more also, if I do not make your life as the life of one of them by this time tomorrow." Then he was afraid, and he arose and ran for his life.
>
> 1 Kings 19:1–3

When my kids were little, my favorite story to tell them was Elijah and the prophets of Baal, complete with dramatic pauses, sound effects, and plenty of theatrics.

In the story, God's prophet Elijah has a showdown with 450 prophets of the false god Baal. God's people had been tempted to leave him to worship this other deity, and Elijah was over it. He proposed a showdown. Elijah would prepare a sacrifice to God, and Baal's prophets would prepare one for their god. Whichever god sent fire down on the sacrifice was the real God.

Elijah let the other prophets go first. For hours, they cried out to Baal, even cutting themselves to try to get his attention. All they got in return was radio silence. Elijah even began to taunt them, wondering out loud if Baal was on the porcelain throne and couldn't help out. (Seriously. Check out 1 Kings 18:27.)

After spending almost a whole day waiting, Elijah got his turn. He built an altar, then dug a trench around it. He directed people to dump vessel after vessel of water on the altar until the trench filled with the runoff. He prayed for God to answer, and fire dramatically fell from the sky. It not only burned up the offering but the entire altar and the water as well.

Empowered by the victory, Elijah and the Israelites slayed the 450 false prophets. It was an incredible sight, and it turned Israel back to their God. That is, except for Ahab and Jezebel, the evil king and queen who were quite fond of Baal and none too happy with Elijah.

Despite Elijah's tremendous victory in 1 Kings 18, the opening verses in 1 Kings 19 find him running for his life and sinking into a deep depression. It's almost as if he's forgotten the fire from heaven and the power of the God he serves. It's comforting to me, actually. Valleys follow mountaintops, and when I'm feeling down, I'm in the company of godly prophets.

Elijah's stand against the false prophets is one of the Bible's best examples of taking a minority position (and trash talking). As you learn to step into the minority positions God puts in front of you, you will find more and more opportunities to keep going. Some of them will be great successes, like Elijah's victory. And sometimes you'll drop the touchdown pass in the end zone. Or you'll miss the obvious opportunity in front of you. Or fear will drive you to do something that would have seemed impossible just a day before.

When that happens, keep going.

Elijah might have fled to a cave in fear, but God wasn't finished with him. He sent food and water to reenergize Elijah. God spoke kindly to him. And, most importantly, God trusted him with another assignment.

Each minority position is an opportunity to reengage with the work God is doing. Your successes and failures of the past don't matter as much as your obedience today.

Keep going. Even the greatest prophets had off days.

Prayer

God, it's comforting to see that the spiritual greats weren't immune to fear, mistakes, or confusion. No matter my success or failure rate in the past, I'm looking for a minority position you put in front of me today. When I recognize it, I will take action and not run away. Amen.

Get in the Game

1. Where in your life are your past successes or failures tempting you to give up and run away? Pick a small way to reengage that issue today, trusting God to meet you in the process.

   OR

2. After running away from Jezebel, Elijah stopped in the wilderness. He was at the end of his rope and asked God to take away his life. God responded by giving Elijah a nap. When he woke from that, he ate some food delivered by an angel. Sometimes a nap and a snack are what we need to reorient ourselves. Find a time this week to catch a nap during the day, or choose a night when you can turn in early and get at least two extra hours of sleep. Notice how this influences your mood and productivity the next day.

DAY 28

THREEFOLD CORD
MEN ARE TEAM PLAYERS

> And though a man might prevail against one who is alone, two will withstand him—a threefold cord is not quickly broken.
>
> Ecclesiastes 4:12

It is common to hear this bit of biblical wisdom read at wedding ceremonies. It is a good verse with application to marriage, but it isn't really about that. It is about strength in numbers. Marriage is one way to find this strength. Friends and family are another.

There are things in life that I can't handle on my own. Some I need my wife for. Some I need a good friend for. And some are so big they require the investment of many brothers.

The book of Ecclesiastes is focused on exposing the vanities of life—the things that we strive for but find lacking when we finally grasp them. This Scripture points to one of those: it is vanity to assume that I am enough on my own. That might cause the self-help gurus to bristle, but it's the truth. I can't think of a single problem in life that wouldn't have been lessened by the help of the right person at the right time. I actually don't have to do it all on my own. Personal development and emotional growth are great, but they won't lead us to a life that endures and wins. We need others in the fight with us to get there.

The key to building a threefold cord is to ask—you never know what may lead to a binding and strengthening friendship. This has played out again and again in my own life.

There is a 1978 Jeep CJ7 in my garage. I am in the process of doing a full restomod on it. That means I'm restoring it to its former glory while also making some choice modifications. I took the entire thing down to the rusted frame. Every surface has been rehabbed and repainted. Every single nut and bolt has passed between my fingers. When I run into snags in the project that I can't complete on my own—and there have been plenty—I have go-to friends chomping at the bit to lend a hand. I wouldn't be anywhere near where I am now without their expertise.

Earlier this year, when I fell behind on a project the city was requiring at my house, it was friends who came to help me dig post holes and build a breezeway connecting my home and garage. I wouldn't have hit the deadline without them.

I just returned from a monthlong excursion through Canada and Alaska. I camped for thirty days and drove over nine thousand miles, reaching as far north as the Arctic Circle. It was an incredible experience, and one that was heightened because I had three other couples, good friends, along for the ride. Every high was even higher and every challenge was lessened simply because they were there.

Men dream of being self-sufficient. There is something noble about wanting to take care of yourself and not be a burden to others. However, real strength lies in numbers. Lone wolves are weaker and die sooner than those that run in a pack.

When you are in a pinch financially, who can you call? When a pipe bursts and you need an extra set of hands willing to work, who will you ask? When your marriage hits a pothole and you need a listening ear and wise counsel, where can you turn? When you are experiencing death by paper cut and you need some fun in your life, what friend will jump in with you?

You are not enough on your own. That's actually a good thing. It means you have space for great friends. Choose and invest wisely, and they will take your life to the next level.

All you have to do is start. It's as simple and difficult as that.

Prayer

God, I am grateful for this wisdom. I don't want to move through life on my own. I want to receive help from a team, and I want to give help too. Show me how to do that today. I am grateful that you have designed us to need each other. That is not a weakness but a strength. Amen.

Get in the Game

1. Think back on your life. When you were in crisis or just needed help on a project, who did you call? If you can think of names, reach out to those guys today and express your gratitude. Want to kick it up a notch? Venmo them some drink money as a sign of your appreciation.

     OR

2. If you look hard enough, there is likely something in your life you could use help on, whether it's changing your brakes or overcoming emotional pain. Ask God who can help you with this. Whatever name comes to mind, reach out to them today and ask. It's an incredibly vulnerable and risky move—which means it's the path to breakthrough and it will please God.

DAY 29

THE THINGS WE DON'T WANT TO DO
MEN WORK

> Then Simon Peter, having a sword, drew it and struck the high priest's servant and cut off his right ear. (The servant's name was Malchus.) So Jesus said to Peter, "Put your sword into its sheath; shall I not drink the cup that the Father has given me?"
>
> John 18:10–12

I call BS on the people who claim, "If you have a job you love, you'll never work a day in your life." That nugget of so-called wisdom only leaves us second-guessing when we run into the reality of work. By its nature, work is difficult, especially in the early stages of your career. Even if you love it, there will be challenges, headaches, and days when you want to give up. This has been true for me, and it was true for Jesus.

While we're at it, let's call BS on the people who claim Jesus was against weapons too. He didn't crack on Peter carrying a sword for self-defense. Instead, he criticized its use in this specific situation. Why? Because Peter was trying to stop Jesus from his God-given task. He was standing in the way of Christ's most important work.

Right before this scene, after a night of prayer, Jesus had made peace with his death. So stressed that he was sweating blood, Jesus basically said to his Father, "I don't want to do this. Please let this cup pass from me. But if you want me to do it, I will accomplish your will before having my preferred outcome."

When Peter stepped in, sword in hand, to pursue his own agenda, Jesus shut him down. Jesus had already won the battle in his mind to go forward with the task the Father had given him. Not even his well-meaning friends could stop him from that work.

Do I expect work to be easy? Do I lash out when I experience challenges? Do I run toward the problems as Jesus did, or do I run away? Do I preserve my preferred way of life or alter it for the purpose of God?

A mark of our love for God is our willingness to work—to do the things we don't want to do. This is true everywhere you will go today: at the office, at home, and everything in between. It's no surprise, then, that willingness to work is also a key to a long-term, healthy marriage. Fortunately, marriage stuff is usually only mildly unpleasant, like taking out the garbage or visiting the in-laws for a weekend. But the call of God is for much larger stakes and often requires much larger sacrifices.

It is hard work to stay married, and it is hard work to follow God, which is why so many people choose not to do either. Jesus wasn't married, but he was wedded to the mission of God and resolute on seeing it played out. That mission cost him his life, and it also bought mine.

Not everyone will understand the tasks God calls you to complete or the work he calls you to do. Push forward anyway.

Breakthrough could be waiting on the other side of your resolve.

Prayer

Jesus, you have unparalleled strength, resolve, and tenacity. I want to be more like you. When you call me to do something, I want to see it through to completion. Whatever you put before me today I will work at wholeheartedly. Amen.

Get in the Game

1. Hundreds of years before Jesus was born, the prophet Isaiah spoke about the Messiah's tenacity to accomplish God's tasks, describing him as having set his face "like a flint" (Isa. 50:7). Find a rock and keep it in your pocket all day. When you are tempted to take the easy road, let it remind you to also set your face like a flint and work.

   OR

2. Is there something God is pushing you to do that you've been putting off? If so, take a concrete step toward it today. If not, willingly choose to do a task at home, the office, or with friends that you don't normally want to do—let it build your muscle memory for the next time God calls you to a difficult task.

DAY 30

LIVE ABOVE THE NOISE
MEN ARE PROTECTORS

> And I heard a loud voice in heaven, saying, "Now the salvation and the power and the kingdom of our God and the authority of his Christ have come, for the accuser of our brothers has been thrown down, who accuses them day and night before our God."
>
> Revelation 12:10

The accuser mentioned in this verse is Satan. This picture of his eventual defeat at the hands of God has not occurred yet. In the meantime, we should still expect him to come against us the same way he always has: with accusations. This is key to his plan to take us out.

Protectors have outward-facing vision. They put the needs of others before their own needs. They lay their life on the line for the vulnerable. They bring a sense of strength and comfort. Satan comes against that by looking to turn our vision inward instead.

The Evil One wants me fixated on my problems and past pain. He wants me to live a life of guilt and regret. He wants me licking my wounds. When I'm looking backward and inward, I'll never be able to move forward and recognize the opportunities that lie ahead.

It may sound shocking, but sin isn't necessarily Satan's goal. All he needs to do is sideline us. If a sin can do that, then he will strike. If he can't entice us into a mistake, he will try to paralyze us with accusations.

I'm listening to the voice of the accuser when . . .

I feel I am not measuring up.

I feel guilty about mistakes I've already apologized for.

I remember times I failed as a husband or dad.

I carry regret for past financial decisions.

I dwell on costly relational mistakes.

I play the "what if" game of reimagining my life.

I second-guess choices I can no longer change.

I struggle to believe God has forgiven my mistakes.

I replay missed opportunities to be a protector.

The spiritually mature have to live above the noise of the accuser. We do this by choosing to believe Jesus has once and for all set us free from our past. His sacrifice covers us and everything we have ever done. End of story.

The Bible says that "we love because he first loved us" (1 John 4:19). I believe the same is true for protectors. We protect because Jesus first protected us. His life, death, and resurrection were acts of protection, and they remain the antidote to the accuser's poison.

To be effective, protectors have to leave behind the crippling accusations of the past. Yesterday does not define me. It's what I do today that sets the course of my life.

We can listen to God's voice or we can dwell on Satan's accusations, but we cannot do both.

Prayer

Father, I am sorry for the times I live with my eyes on the rearview mirror. I want to focus on the steps you are calling me to take, not the successes or failures of my past. I fix my eyes forward on you today. I will answer the call to protect. Amen.

Get in the Game

1. Secrets lose their power when they're shared. As an act of defiance against the accuser, get in touch with a trusted friend and share a regret you are having trouble moving past. Finish by asking them to pray for you.

   OR

2. Revelation 21:5 says God is making all things new. This includes you. Write the word *new* on your wrist today and use it as a reminder to keep your life (and mind) forward-focused. Look for new protector opportunities today and jump on them.

WEEK
7

DAY 31

MOVING FORWARD
MEN HAVE A VISION

> For it has seemed good to the Holy Spirit and to us to lay
> on you no greater burden than these requirements: that you
> abstain from what has been sacrificed to idols, and from
> blood, and from what has been strangled, and from sexual
> immorality. If you keep yourselves from these, you will do
> well.
>
> Acts 15:28–29

This story from Acts 15, and these verses in particular,
is very freeing to me. I sometimes feel like I am missing
something because I don't always have clear direction from
the Lord. To hear some people talk, it's as if God directs
them on which socks to wear each morning. It is not that
way with me, and apparently it wasn't that way for the early
church leaders and apostles either.

The first followers of Jesus were all adherents of the ancient Jewish faith. That meant they had been taught to keep
and live by the 613 laws extracted from the Old Testament.

When Christianity began to spread to the Gentiles, these new believers were genuinely confused. Did they have to keep all these laws too? Did they have to eat kosher? Did they have to be circumcised as adults?

These Gentile believers asked Peter and the apostles for clarity. This was no small issue. Yet the early church leaders didn't stall, waiting for irrefutable proof from God. They prayed about it, discussed it, and then did what seemed best to them and the Holy Spirit. That was enough to keep moving.

I make decisions every day that seem good to me and seem like something the Holy Spirit would be okay with. That's good enough. While there are some times of unmistakable spiritual clarity, they are rare. Most days require a degree of faith to keep moving.

Someone once said to me, "Just because it is a good idea doesn't mean it is a God idea." Why not? God is good. This life is about walking by faith, not waiting for turn-by-turn instructions from on high. If you're waiting for certainty, you'll likely stay stalled.

God has given us the Holy Spirit as a guide and the freedom to move our life forward under his direction the best we know how.

Good enough is good enough—let's keep moving.

Prayer

Lord, I am invigorated—and also a bit intimidated—by the freedom you give. I want to serve you and get things right. I am thankful there is grace when I don't and that you are pleased more in my trying than in my waiting. Please help me and grow my vision. Amen.

Get in the Game

1. Where have you been stalling on your vision? Decide how you can take a step to move it forward today, then execute on it. Visions that stop moving die.

   OR

2. Jesus said the Holy Spirit would be a guide that leads you into all truth (John 16:13). He is the X factor to a life that works, but he is too often left on the sidelines. Every time you eat today, ask the Holy Spirit to guide you. When you feel a nudge to do or say something the Holy Spirit would be okay with, do it. Even if you get it wrong, God will be pleased with your attempt to engage with the Spirit.

DAY 32

THROW A PUNCH AT ANXIETY
MEN TAKE MINORITY POSITIONS

> Do not be anxious about anything, but in everything by
> prayer and supplication with thanksgiving let your requests
> be made known to God.
>
> Philippians 4:6

"Do not be anxious about anything" have to be some of the
most anti-American words in all of Scripture. Our culture
feeds us anxiety as a way of life. We have grown so accus-
tomed to it, we hardly even notice it anymore. Anxiety has
become the background music to our days.

We could blame the 24/7 news cycle, which uses anxiety as a hook to keep us coming back. We could blame
social media, which uses the fear of missing out to keep
us scrolling. We could blame the economy, which has all
of us feeling less secure with our financial future than we
ever imagined. We could blame the other political party or

inflation or the cost of living or . . . or . . . or . . . The list goes on and on.

Anxiety is not a uniquely American experience. It was obviously an issue for Paul and other believers in the first century, or else the words of today's Scripture would never have been written. That being said, we are arguably the most anxiety-prone generation in all of world history. We have more phobias, medications, insurance policies, savings for rainy days, and mental illnesses than Paul could have imagined. Yet Paul's antidote still works: prayer and thanksgiving. It not only counteracts our current anxiety, it will keep us from becoming anxious in the future.

Instead of practicing the American way of being stressed about everything possible, I'm prompted to praise God through gratitude. This isn't choosing to wear rose-colored glasses. Gratitude is actually more grounded in reality than anxiety has ever been. Anxiety focuses on what could be, while gratitude looks at what God has already done. One is focused on a future that might not happen, while the other chooses to see the blessings already present.

It is physically impossible to be both anxious and grateful at the same time. It is like flipping a light switch in a dark room. Gratitude causes anxiety to run.

In a world powered by constant anxiety, gratitude is a minority position. It is an anchor point and a foundation on which we can build a life of peace.

"Do not be anxious about anything" starts right now:

God, I thank you for allowing me to see a full moon last night, which was lovely. I recognize the server we had at dinner had great and commendable character. Thank you for allowing me to see you in her. I am thankful for my friend who has gone ninety days without any alcohol on his journey to recovery. I am thankful for time spent camping with my wife. I am thankful for our dog that brings me joy. I am thankful for physical protection in a car wreck last year. I am thankful to do work that is meaningful around people who let me be me.

Today, choose gratitude, and throw a punch at anxiety.

Prayer

God, anxiety is not meant to be the center point of my life. That position belongs to you. When I am tempted to sit in that fear, bring me back to gratitude. There is so much you have already blessed me with, and when I focus on that, the could-be fears start to fade. You are good to me. Amen.

Get in the Game

1. Set a timer for three minutes and spend that time thanking God for whatever comes to mind: the big things, the small things, and everything in between. There is nothing too insignificant.

   OR

2. Open a new note on your phone and start a gratitude list. Start with the first ten things that come to mind, whatever they are. The next time you are prompted to feel anxious, open the note, read through it, and then spend time adding to it. Consider this ever-growing list an ongoing prayer of gratitude to God. He will be pleased and you will be helped.

DAY 33

FOLLOWERS OVER FANBOYS
MEN ARE TEAM PLAYERS

> And many spread their cloaks on the road, and others
> spread leafy branches that they had cut from the fields.
> And those who went before and those who followed were
> shouting, "Hosanna! Blessed is he who comes in the name
> of the Lord! Blessed is the coming kingdom of our father
> David! Hosanna in the highest!"
>
> Mark 11:8–10

If you are a team player, I can guarantee one thing will
eventually happen: decisions will be made that you don't
agree with. It is then that you get to practice the uncomfortable and unsexy work of submitting to authority.

That last sentence has two curse words to most Americans: the *S* word and the *A* word—though not the ones
you're probably thinking of. I'm talking about *submit* and
authority.

In a culture whose highest ideal is personal "freedom," anything that slightly resembles doing something we don't want to do rubs us like sandpaper. Yet you cannot be a functioning and contributing member of a team, chasing a vision larger than your own glory, if you can't submit to authority. Championship teams are led by a coach whom all players slot themselves under. It's the same with Jesus.

In this scene from Mark 11, which happens just a few days before the crucifixion, Jesus enters Jerusalem to great fanfare. He seems to be on top of the world, but the people gathered aren't necessarily celebrating who he is. They are celebrating their personal agenda that they expect him to fulfill.

During the Maccabean revolt two centuries earlier, Jews had taken a stand against Greek culture and the ever-encroaching Seleucid empire. Godless emperors had taken the promised land, defiled the Jewish temple, and worked to secularize the society. The Jews, led by Judas Maccabeus, fought back. The palm branch was a sort of flag and symbol of this rebellion. It was so tied to Israel's national identity that it would later be used on their currency.

As he enters Jerusalem, Jesus isn't being fanned by palm branches to cool him down on a sweltering day. Rather, the crowd is waving their flag and putting its nationalist agenda on him. They expect Jesus to rally the troops and lead a rebellion to overthrow Rome, the dominating world power of the day.

Most of us have our own palm branches, agendas that we put on Jesus rather than seeking out and submitting to his agenda. It seems every subculture has their own Jesus. People on the right have their favorite Bible verses that seem to bolster their position, as do people on the left. Capitalists justify their money fixation because of all the times Jesus mentions money, and social justice warriors have their verses as to why wealth should be shared. There seems to be no shortage of personal Jesuses: environmentalist Jesus and business-first Jesus, live-and-let-live hippie Jesus and turn-or-burn Jesus. I could go on and on.

We have to be very careful not to be a fanboy of Jesus just because we think he agrees with us or because we think he is going to fulfill our agenda. He will have none of that.

It was common for military heroes to ride into conquered towns on warhorses as a show of strength and bravado. Jesus enters Jerusalem on a donkey not just to fulfill a prophecy but to send a message that he will not be anyone's culture warrior. He has one agenda: God's.

Most of us are still in the crowd, waving our preferred palm branch and looking to coax Jesus to our side. The real power lies in leaving the crowd behind and filing in behind Jesus, submitting to his agenda and authority.

Jesus isn't looking for fanboys. He wants followers.

Prayer

Jesus, I am sorry for the times that I have put my agenda on you. You are much bigger than my pre-ferred way of life, my preferred political candidate, or my preferred worship experience. Today, I choose to put down my palm branch and follow you. I submit myself to whatever your agenda is for me today. Put me in, Coach, I'm ready to play. Amen.

Get in the Game

1. A prayer I regularly pray is "God, whatever you have going on today, I want to be part of it." Speak that prayer out loud to God, then go about your day with your eyes open and your muscles primed to jump into action. When you see something that God might be behind, jump in and get your hands dirty.

     OR

2. If you have trouble submitting to earthly authority, you will have trouble submitting to the spiritual authority of God. Today, make it a point to be a blessing to someone in authority over you. Don't be a brownnoser, but be the type of person you would want to lead. Read Hebrews 13:17 if you need motivation to get started.

DAY 34

MILK AND MEAT
MEN WORK

> Though by this time you ought to be teachers, you need
> someone to teach you again the basic principles of the
> oracles of God. You need milk, not solid food. . . . But solid
> food is for the mature, for those who have their powers of
> discernment trained by constant practice to distinguish
> good from evil.
>
> Hebrews 5:12, 14

As a preacher and teacher, I kind of wish this section of
Scripture didn't exist. Not because I disagree with it and
not because it isn't incredibly helpful. What I don't like is
how it gets misused.

Nearly every follower of Christ I know would self-identify
as "the mature." They think of themselves as ready and capable of handling solid food. Let me pull off the Band-Aid:
most of us are still feeding on milk. I can tell by the way we
live.

Solid food, or "meat" in other translations, isn't about hearing a deep spiritual teaching you've never encountered before. When I preach, I want to be compelling and winsome. Jim Rayburn, who started a ministry to students called Young Life, said, "It is a sin to bore people with the gospel." But Bible teaching isn't meant to be merely entertainment or mental stimulation. We hear teaching, read Scripture, and pray so that we can practice what is good and avoid what is evil. In other words, we learn so that we can do.

We prove that we are immature when we want new teaching before applying the prior teaching we received. Have you been a Christian for ten years, or are you a Christian who keeps reliving the first year for ten years running? Teaching isn't a spiritual stand-up routine—it's meant to stimulate new actions.

When you hear a teaching on prayer, there isn't any need to be taught anything additional until you actually develop a prayer life. When God teaches us about finances, he doesn't need to teach us anything else until we learn to tithe, get out of debt, and begin to save. When we hear the Sermon on the Mount, we have plenty of action points to implement—we don't need some cutting-edge teaching on dramatic spiritual gifts or the return of Christ.

In Luke 6:46, Jesus taught that the proof of our sincerity lies in what we do: "Why do you call me 'Lord, Lord,' and not do what I tell you?"

It is only when we receive and apply the basic teachings of Jesus—the milk—that we qualify ourselves for the next level of information from God. I wish the writer of Hebrews would have spelled out some specific examples of what is meant by "milk" and "meat." I have a hunch they aren't what some of us think.

One of those basic milk teachings for me is Philippians 2:12: "Work out your own salvation." Just like pumping iron grows my muscles and improves my health, my faith grows when I put in reps doing the things Jesus commands. Things like loving God, practicing obedience to his promptings, praying for my enemies, being a blessing to others, and displaying generosity all align with the heart of God. They are milk that will lead to meat. I am committed to working out my salvation by practicing them today.

Prayer

God, I do not need more mental stimulation, I need to move my muscles in obeying your commands. Give me an opportunity to do that today and I am committed to taking it. I will put in the reps with milk until you see fit to give me meat. I trust your ways. Amen.

Get in the Game

1. What is a "milk" teaching of Christ you are having trouble implementing in your life? Spend time asking God to give you opportunities for growth in that area, then commit to taking the next one that finds you. Work out your faith now and it will pay dividends in the future.

   OR

2. Take fifteen minutes and read the Sermon on the Mount in Matthew 5–7 (yes, all of it). As you read, look for a teaching from Jesus that you can work into your life today. Go and make it happen before the sun goes down. You are putting yourself on the path to meat. Well done.

DAY 35

THE CHORUS OF THE COMFORTABLE
MEN ARE PROTECTORS

> Thus says the LORD of hosts: These people say the time has
> not yet come to rebuild the house of the LORD.
>
> Haggai 1:2

Protectors are action-oriented. When they see a problem,
they don't form a committee. They don't deep-dive into research for a month. They don't dip their toe into the water
to see how it feels. They move.

Haggai was a prophet at a difficult time in Israel's history.
After living seventy years in exile in a foreign land, God's
people had begun to trickle back to their homeland. Instead
of rebuilding the temple and setting a strong spiritual foundation for the nation, the people were most concerned with
their own homes, fields, and businesses.

They had turned inward. Instead of being protectors with an eye toward building a better future for their struggling nation, they'd become predators focused on filling their own bellies and pockets. Years passed and the temple continued to lie in ruins.

Their excuse? The time had not yet come. This remains the motto for every unfaithful person across generations. It's the chorus that the comfortable sing over and over. It is a song for boys.

It is a sad reality that predators get most of the headlines, but I believe there are actually more protectors in the world than we realize. Men are drawn to this role. It is why we respect protectors in the military and law enforcement and why we are drawn to superheroes and action movies. For the majority of men, the issue is not convincing us to be protectors—we already want to do that. The hurdle is time.

We want to be a physical protector . . . but we'll get the brakes fixed on the family car next week when we have more free time.

We want to be a spiritual protector . . . but we'll start praying for others tomorrow when we haven't overslept.

We want to be a relational protector . . . but this month is really busy at work. Maybe we'll find time for friends when this project is finished.

We want to be a financial protector . . . but we'll wait until we get a raise to start saving money.

We don't normally outright disagree with God's direction, we just think the time isn't now. It will be better later.

Later, when I have guarantees. Later, when I've built up more savings. Later, when I'm in a better relational space. Later, when I've been able to put down roots. Later, when I'm not so stressed. Later, when the business takes off. Later, when . . .

There will never be a "later" opportunity for unfaithful people. That is only reached when we courageously and unselfishly plow forward in doing the things we know God would approve of right now.

In the heart of the struggle for civil rights, Dr. Martin Luther King Jr., speaking to graduates at Oberlin College, echoed Haggai's call to action:

> Let nobody give you the impression that the problem of racial injustice will work itself out. Let nobody give you the impression that only time will solve the problem. That is a myth, and it is a myth because time is neutral. It can be used either constructively or destructively . . . the time is always right to do right.[1]

You don't become a protector by accident. Time will not just work itself out. It is what you do that sets your path in life.

Protectors don't say "later." The time is always right to do right. And the time is now.

Prayer

God, I don't want to stall. I don't want to sing along with the comfortable who want to put off what they should do for another day. Being a protector is a challenge, but it is the path to a potent life of meaning. I enter today with a protector mindset. I will follow you and your promptings. Amen.

Get in the Game

1. Where in your life have you been saying "the time has not yet come"? Spend some time considering why you've been dragging your feet and what it has cost you. Now go and get the ball rolling. There's no need to wait any longer.

   OR

2. Protectors are primed to move. Put that into practice today by intentionally being the first to jump in. That might mean sharing first in a meeting, doing the dishes without being asked, or getting to the gym extra early. This will build quick-response muscle for the next protector opportunity you come across.

WEEK
8

DAY 36

PRESS ON
MEN HAVE A VISION

> Now when the adversaries of Judah and Benjamin heard
> that the returned exiles were building a temple to the LORD,
> the God of Israel, . . . [they] discouraged the people of
> Judah and made them afraid to build and bribed counselors
> against them to frustrate their purpose.
>
> Ezra 4:1, 4–5

What is at the heart of every vision? Difficulty and
opposition.

There are no shortcuts to vision, even if you are the people
of God and the vision is pure and supported by him—like
rebuilding his temple after it was laid to waste by an enemy
army.

Their difficulty in executing this vision was not just due to
the logistics of getting building materials and finding skilled
labor. They also had flesh-and-blood enemies endlessly trying to stop them.

If God's ancient people encountered massive opposition to their efforts, why am I surprised when I do? If they were discouraged, why shouldn't I be from time to time? If they had doubts and yet pressed on through endless roadblocks, why shouldn't I do the same? If people came against the vision of God in the Bible, then why am I surprised when people come against what God is asking me to do today?

It was a long road, but God's people pressed on and got the temple reconstructed. I am encouraged by their tenacity in the face of opposition, and I want to emulate them.

Vision is important, but ultimately life isn't about that. It's bigger than any idea, goal, building, or organization. Life is about doing what I sense God wants me to do. Faithfulness to him in pursuing the visions he has given me is even more important than actually accomplishing those visions.

He is looking for men who will press on through difficulty and opposition. I choose to be one of them.

Prayer

God, I am honored and humbled that you would give me visions to pursue. I am sorry for the times I have let discouragement stop me. I vow to press on today and take a tangible step toward something you have called me to do. Amen.

Get in the Game

1. Where have you been listening to the voices and opinions of scoffers and discouragers around your vision? Get distance from them today and press forward as an act of faith.

   OR

2. Galatians 6:9 says, "Let us not grow weary of doing good, for in due season we will reap, if we do not give up." Work on committing this verse to memory and let it push you forward when you get discouraged.

DAY 37

ENJOY YOUR FREAKIN' LIFE
MEN TAKE A MINORITY POSITION

> There is an evil that I have seen under the sun, and it lies
> heavy on mankind: a man to whom God gives wealth, pos-
> sessions, and honor, so that he lacks nothing of all that he
> desires, yet God does not give him power to enjoy them.
> . . . This is vanity; it is a grievous evil.
>
> Ecclesiastes 6:1–2

Solomon, the author of Ecclesiastes, has all of the things
listed in this passage: wealth, possessions, and honor. He
has everything anyone would want, except one thing: a life
he enjoys. He calls out to all of us who have spiritual bearings in the twenty-first century to learn from his mistakes.

Do not be caught up in the rat race. Do not measure your
life against everyone else's. Do not think getting ahead
financially is actually moving you forward. Do not think
that more promotions, more accomplishments, and more

recognition will finally bring you peace. Many people have all those things and more, yet like Solomon, they still haven't figured out how to have a life they enjoy. So they keep chasing, they keep getting, but they never arrive.

Believe it or not, God wants you to enjoy your life—the one you have right now. It is called "good stewardship."

Years ago, I would never have believed I would write that last sentence. I would have said that seeking to enjoy your life is for godless hedonists. I believed that to understand the cause of Christ is to constantly suffer and to have fun only by accident. God does call me to sacrifice, but he does not call me to save the world. That is his job. He does call me to pick up my cross and be willing to die every day, but he does not call me to intentionally run myself into the ground. That would intentionally destroy his creation.

If my son only worked and worked, ignoring his friends and family, it would break my heart. If my son never laughed or rode his motorcycle or joined me on a camping trip, it would bring me down. If my son achieved the highest rung on the corporate ladder but didn't enjoy the life he'd built, I would be crushed.

This is the same with God. Yes, he is a king with standards and plans and expectations for each of us. But he is also a loving father who smiles when his children enjoy the lives he has blessed us with.

It is a problem when our soul is not satisfied with life's good things. It is a problem when we live to give our children a good life but forget about ourselves (Eccles. 6:3). It is a problem when messages like this sound like heresy to modern Christians. Maybe that is why our lives don't look attractive to most unbelievers. Maybe that is why we have the same burnout and psychological issues as atheists. Maybe that is why joy is a theoretical concept but not a lived reality for many of us.

Pleasure is a gift from God. It takes revenge against all the petty pain in life. Fun is not frivolous. It is an essential minority position that more men need to take.

Learn from the wisdom of Solomon and go enjoy your freakin' life.

Prayer

Lord, I am thankful for your ways and for your wisdom that transcends time. You have generously given me so many good gifts. I want to enjoy them today and bring a smile to your face. You are a good King and a good Father. I am honored to be called your son. Amen.

Get in the Game

1. What is something you love to do? If you haven't done it in the last seven days, then you're seriously overdue for some fun. Adjust your schedule and make time for it this week. When you are tempted to wait, don't. God wants you to enjoy your life. It is that important, so make it a priority. Bonus points if you bring along someone else.

   OR

2. Open yourself to a difficult conversation by asking someone close to you (spouse, friend, family member) where they see you overextending yourself. Listen to their response and resist the urge to defend yourself. Consider what they say, and if necessary, make adjustments to how you spend your time and effort.

DAY 38

TO THE NEXT LEVEL
MEN ARE TEAM PLAYERS

> And those who are wise shall shine like the brightness of
> the sky above; and those who turn many to righteousness,
> like the stars forever and ever.
>
> Daniel 12:3

Other than being in alignment with the Scriptures, nothing
is a more solid predictor of a successful life than having the
right friends. We become who we spend time with.

Want to elevate your prayer life? Choose friends who pray
and then see things happen. Want to get ahead financially?
Get friends who manage their money better than you do.
Need a breakthrough in your marriage? Find friends who
know how to treat their spouse, have fun together, and
work through conflict.

The Old Testament book of Daniel is rare among the books
of the Bible in that it is split right down the middle. The
first half of the book is narrative, telling the familiar stories

of Daniel interpreting dreams, surviving the lions' den, and supporting his friends Hananiah, Mishael, and Azariah (known more commonly by their Babylonian names of Shadrach, Meshach, and Abednego).

The second half of the book drops the stories and focuses on prophecy. Daniel recounts dreams and visions of things that will take place in the future, including angelic conflicts and the downfall of great empires. The prophecies in Daniel are pretty astounding, and many of them have already been fulfilled. But I find myself getting bogged down in prophecy. It often gets me guessing at the outcome or what is meant by the imagery, and it causes me to turn inward. What really gets my attention are verses like Daniel 12:3.

One of the through lines in Daniel, found in his stories and his prophecies, is the importance of people. Daniel is one of the mightiest men of God in the entire Bible, and we find him deriving his strength from his friends. When kidnapped and taken to Babylon, Daniel and his friends worked together to keep their Jewish identity and faith (Dan. 1:8–16). They rose up the ranks together because of God's faithfulness (1:17–21). And when Daniel needed to interpret the king's dream, he ran to his friends and asked them to pray for his success (2:17).

Daniel thrived in a challenging situation, living as an exile serving godless king after godless king, because he was relationally connected. Contrast that with men today, floundering despite our comfortable lives because we are relationally disconnected. It is why so many social indicators of health and wholeness are in the toilet.

I shudder to think where I would be without Dave in high school, Eric in college, Denny as a guiding force for decades, my deep bench of dudes on Thursday mornings, the guys I hunt with and ride motorcycles with, and the close friends I've worked alongside for decades.

Let's not let this world delude us, and instead let's listen to Daniel. Wisdom is understanding that the most important thing I can do with my time is to be with people. It makes me shine relationally, emotionally, and spiritually. It also gives me the opportunity to impact the lives of others and turn them "to righteousness."

Our bank accounts will shrink. Our health will fade. Our country will eventually fall just like Babylon did. The goals that come with the American dream will not ultimately or eternally last. But the team players, those who value and build people, will shine like the stars and not be extinguished.

The lives of spiritual greats like Daniel went to the next level because of their friendships. I will choose to walk that same path.

Prayer

God, people are among your greatest gifts to me. Thank you for the friends, mentors, coworkers, and neighbors you have put in my path. Today, I reject the easy passivity of living life alone and accept the challenges and blessings of friendships. I will take a step toward deepening my relational life today. Amen.

Get in the Game

1. Look back on your life and make a mental list of the people who have had the most impact on you—the friends who have elevated you. Choose one you haven't spoken to in a while and reach out to them today. Take time to reconnect, express your gratitude for their influence on your life, and ask if there is anything you can do to support them.

   OR

2. It sounds cliché but it is true: the best way to have friends is to be a friend. Take stock of the people around you today. Who do you notice that could use a friend? The new guy at work? The elderly neighbor? Your kid's baseball coach? Pray for them, then look for an opportunity to strike up a conversation and listen well. Keep making deposits in their life and see what God does with them.

DAY 39

HOLY DIFFICULTY
MEN WORK

> The LORD God took the man and put him in the garden of
> Eden to work it and keep it.
>
> Genesis 2:15

There is such a thing as holy difficulty. It is called work, and
it is essential to the will of God. It's been that way since the
beginning of time.

This verse is taken from the creation story that begins the
Bible. To the surprise of all the boys wanting to stay on
the couch, this verse comes *before* sin is introduced and
makes a mess of God's perfect world. Adam was commissioned with work to do while living in paradise with God.

Did God *need* Adam to pull weeds, cultivate crops, and
tend livestock? No, God is fully capable of taking care of
everything on his own. Rather, Adam needed the work to
give him purpose, build his capacity, and connect him to

God. When we engage work correctly, it does all three of those things.

This is why, thousands of years later, when God's people move into the promised land, God allows some enemies to slip through the cracks.

> Now these are the nations that the LORD left, to test Israel by them, that is, all in Israel who had not experienced all the wars in Canaan. It was only in order that the generations of the people of Israel might know war, to teach war to those who had not known it before. (Judges 3:1–2)

God leaves some work for the next generation of his people to complete. The few warring nations left behind will keep Israel sharp and in shape. God can't afford to have the next generation be soft because they just eat off the table of the previous generation's sacrifices. He can't have them expecting life will always be a cakewalk. He can't have them waiting for the most important things in life instead of working hard for them.

I could make a comment about the current state of culture in America, but this principle is even more resonant when I turn it on myself. This is how my relationship with God has always worked. The more smooth sailing I have, the easier it is to take my eye off the ball. It is then that I am tempted to turn inward and lose my sharp edge. But when I am in a storm, willing to work toward a cause larger than myself and my comfort, I find myself refreshed and more in sync with God.

This is why I recently decided and declared that I'm going to stay in the pressure of my normal day job until I'm seventy. I need the appropriate level of stress and work to keep myself going straight. Men are like pickup trucks. When we don't have a load, we get squirrelly.

God uses all things—difficulty, complexity, and work—to conform us more into the image of his Son (Rom. 8:28–29). Instead of kicking against it or complaining or giving up, I commit to putting in the work to get to the other side.

Work isn't just about what you can get accomplished, it's a spiritual discipline designed by God for your growth. Engage in it and be changed.

Prayer

Lord, I want to see work the way that you do, as another tool in your tool kit to grow me spiritually. I am sorry for the times I have tried to sidestep your design. No matter what work I have before me today, I will engage it with a positive attitude, looking for you. Amen.

Get in the Game

1. What work do you have before you today? How would your attitude or perspective change if you saw it as an opportunity for holy difficulty, something that God is using to change your life for the better? Adopt that attitude today and see how it influences your output.

    OR

2. Where in your life are you avoiding work? It could be at your nine-to-five, fixing a financial mistake, or engaging counseling with your wife. Wherever it is, take a concrete step forward today, trusting that God will use this hard work for your good. If you need a shot of inspiration, read Romans 8:28–29.

DAY 40

MIGHTY MEN
MEN ARE PROTECTORS

> Now these are the chiefs of David's mighty men, who gave
> him strong support in his kingdom, together with all Israel,
> to make him king, according to the word of the LORD con-
> cerning Israel.
>
> 1 Chronicles 11:10

David's mighty men have always intrigued me. We don't
know all their names, and we don't know much about them.
That is par for the course when it comes to people mighty
before God. They don't protect for recognition, accolades,
or fanfare. They just faithfully knock down the things in front
of them, time after time after time.

The mighty men were physical protectors who went to
great lengths to support their nation, defend their king, and
meet his needs. They were the closest thing to a Special
Forces task unit we get in the Bible. Their stories still teach
us what it takes to be a protector today.

1. *Mighty protectors serve authority with zeal.* Although warriors, David's mighty men were servants first. Their focus wasn't on themselves but on their king. Once, when David wished he could have his favorite water from a well in enemy territory, three mighty men broke through the defenses and brought it back for him. That is serving with zeal—not only doing what is asked of us but anticipating needs and blazing new trails. It's what protectors do.

2. *Mighty protectors know their superpower and use it with endurance.* Josheb killed eight hundred men with his spear. Eleazar struck down Philistines until his hand "froze" to his sword. Benaiah prevailed against a lion in a pit on a snowy day. The mighty men knew their superpower was combat, they trained aggressively, and they used that power with great endurance. Mighty protectors don't quit when the fight comes. They know their superpowers, they develop and leverage them, and they endure until the battle is won. (Find more of their exploits in 2 Samuel 23.)

3. *Mighty protectors control their fear.* Shammah, one of the mighty men, defended an open field against the Philistine army. By himself he stood his ground, and "the LORD worked a great victory" (2 Sam. 23:11– 12). Seeing an enemy army charge you would be terrifying. Shammah must have been scared, but he

didn't flee. Mighty men learn to bring fear under their control, trusting that "victory belongs to the LORD" (Prov. 21:31).

4. *Mighty protectors don't search for glory.* I love the end of 2 Samuel 23 because it just lists out the names of thirty-seven guys and then moves on. There isn't "David's Mighty Men Day" or a big parade. We don't know much about most of these guys, but their names are forever recorded as mighty. They weren't interested in personal glory but in doing their duty. They hit their marks every day, and we still feel the ripple effects of their faithfulness.

These mighty men gathered around David to help him with his earthly kingdom. God is still looking for and gathering mighty men for his heavenly kingdom. He wants warriors who will put in the hard work to advance his kingdom and protect those around us. It's what mighty men have always done.

Prayer

Lord, I want to live as a mighty man today. I choose to engage in any battle you send my way. I will serve with zeal, endure the fight, control my fear, and do

so humbly. You are a good king worth serving. Thank
you for enlisting me as a protector. Amen.

Get in the Game

1. Take time to read about David's mighty men in
   2 Samuel 23:8–29. Before you do, ask God to speak
   to you through the passage. After you've read, consider what you think God might be saying to you.
   How can you put that into action today? Go and do
   that thing. You are a mighty man.

   OR

2. Physical protectors defend others and meet their
   tangible needs. Go through your day looking for an
   opportunity either to stand up for someone else or to
   meet a physical need. You might stop coworkers from
   bad-mouthing your manager, give a few dollars to the
   guy on the corner, or fix the front porch light at your
   mom's house. Whatever you do, you are acting as a
   physical protector and slotting yourself in the downline of the mighty men. Well done.

WEEK
9

DAY 41

A GREAT DAY TO DIE
MEN HAVE A VISION

> Truly, truly, I say to you, unless a grain of wheat falls into the earth and dies, it remains alone; but if it dies, it bears much fruit.
>
> John 12:24

This verse makes scientific sense as well as spiritual sense. The things that have gone before eventually must die and become fertilizer for the things that come after. It is easy to recognize this in nature as well as in the life of Christ— without his death, I would have no chance at a meaningful life now or in eternity.

But that doesn't mean embracing this principle is easy. Physical death at the end of life is a reality I am at peace with, but it is the smaller deaths along the way that are harder to take. Dying to bad habits takes work. Dying to misplaced expectations can be excruciating. Dying to myself and serving others might be hardest of all.

Like the seed, these deaths produce new life.

Jesus told his followers to "take up [your] cross and follow me" (Matt. 16:24). Far from a fashion accessory or a monument on a church steeple, a cross was the first century's electric chair. It was a means of execution with a zero percent survival rate. Crosses were heavy, uncomfortable, and designed to increase suffering. We are to mentally, emotionally, and spiritually carry our own execution device so that we can lay down our lives for the cause of Christ at a moment's notice.

A few chapters later, Jesus explains that every person who bears fruit goes through times of pruning—strategic cutting back—in order to bear even more fruit (John 15:1–2). We like the idea of more fruit until we actually experience pruning. It is painful and disorienting. But like the cross, it is the path to life.

When we refuse to let things die or put them on the chopping block ourselves, we risk losing future fruitfulness. Like Paul, I want to be ready and willing to "die every day" (1 Cor. 15:31).

Prayer

Lord, you are God and I am not. You have set this principle in place in both nature and the spirit realm. Even though it can be difficult, I choose to align myself with your reality instead of my preferences. Give me an opportunity to carry my cross today and I will accept it. Amen.

Get in the Game

1. Like weeds in a garden, there are things in your life crowding out and stealing from your visions. Identify one and pull it up by the roots today, allowing it to become fertilizer that pushes your vision to further growth.

   OR

2. Write "15:31" on your bathroom mirror, a reference to Paul's declaration in 1 Corinthians 15:31 that he dies daily. When you see it in the mornings, take a second to look yourself in the eyes and declare out loud, "Today is a great day to die." Then go and find ways to do that.

DAY 42

IN HASTE
MEN TAKE MINORITY POSITIONS

> In this manner you shall eat it: with your belt fastened, your sandals on your feet, and your staff in your hand. And you shall eat it in haste. It is the LORD's Passover.
>
> Exodus 12:11

I have done the traditional Jewish Passover seder meal many times. It can be a special communal experience with spiritual meaning anchored in the history of God's people. But we have to be honest about one thing: that's not how it happened in the Bible.

The original Passover meal that God instituted and the Jews practiced on their last night as slaves in Egypt was meant to be wolfed down as quickly as possible. Why? Because they had to haul ass to freedom as soon as Pharaoh released them. They had miles to cover and a leisurely meal was not on the agenda.

The problem with many of our religious practices today is a focus on internal reflection instead of external action. We'd rather sit around a table and eat than do the hard work of crossing barriers to reach our promised land. A lot of Christians have defaulted to a faith of thinking when God is looking for doers.

When God provides an opportunity, it needs to be jumped on immediately. We don't need days to pray and consider. We don't need graphs, charts, and market research. We need to move.

A friend recently called me and asked if I would pray about loaning him some money. I said, "No, I'm not going to pray." I don't need to pray about helping a brother in need. The Bible has already told me to do that. I just needed to re-lease the funds.

I found out yesterday that I had needlessly hurt someone with my words. Seconds later, I was making two phone calls to apologize and get things straightened out. It was worth stepping out of a meeting to rebuild that relation-ship, and I think my speed honored God (and the person I'd hurt).

I'm not always as successful as in these examples, but my desire is to default to movement as soon as I feel God's prompting. When I know something is the right thing to do, I don't need to weigh my options. I just need to move.

The Passover bread was unleavened because the movement of God's people was going to happen more quickly than it takes a loaf of bread to rise. They were to eat it "in haste," already dressed for the journey ahead.

In a world that defaults to safety and carefully considered choices, movement is a minority position. It is one I wish marked the people of God more than it does. That being said, I will make it my default today.

I am ready to move.

Prayer

God, I am approaching this day with my belt fastened, my sandals on my feet, and my walking stick in hand. I am ready to move. Whatever you prompt me with today, I want to jump on it immediately. You are good and worth the risk. Amen.

Get in the Game

1. Is there something you know you should be doing (or should have done) that you have been putting off? That ends today. You don't need any more time. Start moving on it before the sun sets tonight, trusting God will meet you in that movement.

   OR

2. The Israelites were already dressed for travel before their meal began—they were ready to move. The next time you get dressed, use it as an opportunity to pray. Ask God to put something in your path that you can take immediate action on. When you see it, jump on it. Don't forget your belt—you are going to be moving today.

DAY 43

THE TEAM AT HOME
MEN ARE TEAM PLAYERS

[Joseph] lifted up his eyes and saw his brother Benjamin, his mother's son, and said, "Is this your youngest brother, of whom you spoke to me? God be gracious to you, my son!" Then Joseph hurried out, for his compassion grew warm for his brother, and he sought a place to weep. And he entered his chamber and wept there.

Genesis 43:29–30

When Joseph was a young man, his brothers had faked his death and sold him into slavery. He wound up in Egypt. In a turn of events only God could orchestrate, Joseph went from slave to prisoner to the second-in-command of the world's leading superpower.

At this point in the story, Joseph has more wealth and authority than just about any other man on earth—but family still has the power to make him weep. Laying eyes on a younger brother he hadn't seen in years triggers the pain of estrangement and the loss of intimacy. Looking to keep his identity a secret, he runs off to weep in private.

Statistics around marriage and kids in America are staggering. Pew Research found that, since 1980, the number of people married by age 25 dropped from nearly 66 percent of the US adult population to only 22 percent.[1] Over the same time span, the share of 25-year-olds with children has dropped from 39 percent to 17 percent.[2] US census data shows that half of all states in America are experiencing higher death rates than birth rates.[3]

There are many factors influencing those numbers, but one that none of the pundits will discuss is our culture's loss of wonder around having and enjoying a family. We get engrossed in our careers and give our hearts to success instead of the team at home. We forget the people who were there before our careers or those who will be with us past our retirement. We put off getting married or having kids as long as possible. We look forward to when our kids turn eighteen and we can be "free" again. That is a delusion. Our kids will always want us to be leading and nurturing them. It doesn't matter if they are five years old or thirty-five years old, they want (and need) a dad who is on his game.

Caring for family in any form is a person's highest and most fulfilling calling. God has built us for teams, and your most important one shares your last name.

When God created the world, the only thing he called "not good" was Adam living alone. So he made Eve. Soon thereafter, he blessed the couple with children. I know many men who appear to have life by the throat, accomplishing goals and earning increasing amounts of money, but who, under the veneer, are living a life that is "not good" because it's not focused on anything beyond themselves.

Joseph's tears are a splash of cold water that I need, a reminder to enjoy my family. I should be pouring as much of my time and resources into them as anywhere else. Family is the one thing that will outlast me and go on for generations.

Family comes in all shapes and sizes, but one thing hasn't changed: men are team players who invest in the team at home.

Prayer

Father, I am encouraged that you chose that title for yourself. You are a good Father who has called me into your family. I am grateful for the ways you have invested your time and resources into me. No matter what my family looks like, I want to emulate you and be a blessing to them today. I do this to honor you. Amen.

Get in the Game

1. Go and be the answer to the prayer you just prayed. Find a way to be a blessing to your family today and do it before you hit the sack tonight. Whether it's taking your kid to a park, doing yard work for your parents, or grabbing lunch with your brother, know that your efforts to honor them also honor God.

    OR

2. Because family is such a potent blessing from God, it can also be the place the enemy attacks. If you have a significant pain point from your family, you might need to follow the example of Joseph and take time to weep. That could look like writing out your pain on a piece of paper, sharing it with a trusted friend, finally calling up a counselor, or giving yourself the permission to cry. God promises to be close to the brokenhearted and save those who are crushed in spirit. Use this as an opportunity to draw near to him and find healing (Ps. 34:18).

DAY 44

NOT *FOR* BUT *FROM*
MEN WORK

> In those days Jesus came from Nazareth of Galilee and was
> baptized by John in the Jordan. And when he came up out
> of the water, immediately he saw the heavens being torn
> open and the Spirit descending on him like a dove. And a
> voice came from heaven, "You are my beloved Son; with
> you I am well pleased."
>
> Mark 1:9–11

There are two ways to read this verse and understand what
God the Father says to Jesus. We can hear God saying
something like, "You have done well so I am pleased with
you." This would fit well with our religious obligation sensitivities. Or we can read it more like how the CEB transla-
tion puts it: "You are my Son, whom I dearly love; in you I
find happiness."

If you look closely, you'll notice this story comes in the first
chapter of Mark. We're only nine verses into the whole
thing. At this point, Jesus hasn't done any miracles. He

hasn't given any great teachings. He hasn't called the disciples, turned over tables in the temple, or walked the gruel-
ing path to the cross. This moment happens before anyone
other than Jesus's family and friends knows his name.

The takeaway? Jesus brought God happiness apart from
his work. It rubs against our achieve-to-succeed cultural
mindset, but I believe God feels the same way about you.

You make God happy. He gladly gives you his stamp of
approval—independent of your choices and accomplishments. Until we can believe that, we will never be at peace.
We have to step off the hamster wheel of trying to earn his
love. We already have it.

This feels too good to be true. It sounds like modern, feel-
good psychobabble infiltrating the Bible. So I fired up my
copy of the *Theological Dictionary of the New Testament*,
the premier Biblical Greek dictionary, and took a look. Here
is what it says about that phrase "I am well pleased":[1]

εὐδοκέω (eudokeō)

Verb: To be well-pleased, think it good, be resolved.

21 occurrences in the New Testament:

"Be well pleased" (7x)

"Pleased" (5x)

"Have pleasure" (4x)

"Be willing" (2x)

"Be (one's) good pleasure" (1x)

"Take pleasure" (1x)

"Think good (of)" (1x)

God calls us to work, but his love is not dependent upon it. Jesus had God's approval before he did any meaningful work, and so do you. Instead of working *for* God's approval, you work *from* his approval.

You make God happy. He finds pleasure in being with you. You positively affect his mood. Begin to believe those truths and your work will hit a whole new level.

Prayer

God, you are a good Father! Although it is sometimes hard for me to understand and even to believe that you find pleasure in me, I want to. As I face work today, I want to come at it knowing that I already have your approval instead of trying to earn it. I am your son and I will live like it today. Amen.

Get in the Game

1. What gives you the biggest feeling of pride and accomplishment around your work? A promotion? A position? A big contract or successful project? Here is the truth: God loved you the same the day *before* that happened as he did the day *after* it happened. Whatever work you face today, attack it knowing that you already have God's approval, and notice how believing that truth influences your attitude and demeanor.

   OR

2. God wants to spend time with you because you bring him pleasure. Schedule thirty minutes on your calendar sometime today and spend it with God in a way that also makes you smile. Go for a run, hit your favorite hiking trail, visit an art museum, or sit in your favorite chair with a cold drink. If anything strikes you during your time, write it down and do something about it.

DAY 45

PRIMAL PRACTICES TO SPIRITUAL STRENGTH
MEN ARE PROTECTORS

While Jesus was speaking, a Pharisee asked him to dine
with him, so he went in and reclined at table. The Pharisee
was astonished to see that he did not first wash before dinner. And the Lord said to him, "Now you Pharisees cleanse
the outside of the cup and of the dish, but inside you are
full of greed and wickedness. You fools! Did not he who
made the outside make the inside also?"

Luke 11:37–40

It is not always obvious who the true spiritual protectors
are. It was that way during Jesus's life, and it is still that way
now.

Jesus had some serious chutzpah to give some hard words
to people who'd just invited him to dinner. The religious
leaders were shocked that he didn't wash before mealtime.

This wasn't to remove unsanitary dirt, but rather it was a religious ritual to become ceremonially "clean."

The Pharisees were supposed to be the spiritual protectors of the people of Israel, but Jesus saw through their charade. He pushed them on their motivations. They would wash and do the religious duties that gained them favor in view of others, but they didn't take care of their inner parts that were hidden away.

Rather than being protectors, the Pharisees were living as religious predators. They displayed a holy veneer, but their lives were motivated by pride, recognition, and power more than the movement of God. They used God to get what they wanted rather than being used by God to get what he wanted.

It is easy and addictive to take care of my externals because I get a feeling of fitting in, belonging, and being recognized as good enough. But it is the intangibles—being clean and ordered on the inside—that are the true barometer of how my life is going. If I hope to be a potent spiritual protector, I must be operating from an internal space that is bent toward God. Thankfully, the steps to building that muscle aren't a secret.

Throughout history, protectors have built their spiritual strength through seven primal practices. When done correctly, they won't gain you public acclaim, but they will set you on a course to encounter God.

The 7 Primal Practices

- *Connect with God daily* through Scripture, prayer, and other spiritual disciplines.

- *Receive teaching weekly* through worship services, study groups, and more.

- *Share your story with others* because God's work inside you is powerful.

- *Get baptized* as an external sign of your internal commitment.

- *Join community* because following God is a team sport.

- *Live generously* through tithing and sharing resources because God is generous to us.

- *Serve others* to show God's love and push back against a self-centered culture.

Spiritual protectors understand the need to fall under the protection of God, and they want to bring others with them. I don't want to *look* like a spiritual protector, I want to *live* like one. The seven primal practices ensure that I will.

Prayer

Jesus, I am thankful that you don't let us coast spiritually. No matter how far we have come, there is still more ground to be taken. I commit to do that today by engaging the seven primal practices. Please meet me as I do this and build my spiritual protector muscles. Amen.

Get in the Game

1. Jesus compared the Pharisees to dirty dishes. The next time you use a dish, instead of putting it in the dishwasher, take the time to hand-wash it. You would never consider a bowl or cup clean that was only clean on the outside. As you clean, ask God to reveal any places on the inside that you're neglecting to align with him. If something comes to mind, assume it's from him, then go do something about it.

    OR

2. Look at the list of the seven primal practices. Which one jumps out at you? Why do you think it is gaining your attention, and what can you do to move toward it today? Now go and do that thing. You are building spiritual protector muscles. Well done.

WEEK
10

DAY 46

THE BIG AND THE SMALL
MEN HAVE A VISION

> But since we were torn away from you, brothers, for a
> short time, in person not in heart, we endeavored the more
> eagerly and with great desire to see you face to face. . . .
> For what is our hope or joy or crown of boasting before our
> Lord Jesus at his coming? Is it not you? For you are our
> glory and joy.
>
> 1 Thessalonians 2:17, 19–20

Paul was a man of massive vision. Before him, the epicenter of the Jesus movement (what we now call the church) was located in and around Jerusalem and consisted almost entirely of Jews. Paul's vision, handed to him by God, was to spread it to the corners of the globe, swinging wide the doors to invite people from every nation and people group to join in.

It's hard to know for sure, but Paul himself may have started up to twenty different churches. That number multiplies exponentially when you consider the churches started by men and women he personally mentored.

And, at the same time, he just happened to write the bulk of the New Testament, establishing much of the Christian theology we still live by to this day. How did Paul accomplish so much? He could toggle between a massive macro vision and an intimate micro vision.

One minute Paul was cruising all over the known world, planting churches, inspiring believers, and penning Scripture. The next minute he was in the details of individual lives, praying for their needs, coaching them in faith, and supporting their endeavors. His letters in the Bible are littered with names of people we know very little about today but who were extremely important to him.

Paul wasn't only caught up with the big, he lived for (and invested in) the small.

If your macro vision is causing you to overlook the needs of the people around you, it's time to reassess. The foundation of every vision is other people. Don't sacrifice them for a goal with no heartbeat or breath.

As I get older and leadership gets more complex, I find the urge to focus on the macro goal at the expense of the micro relationship. That's why Paul is compelling to me. At every age, he found the energy for the big and the small.

This is one reason why he was such a blessing to the kingdom of God and why his influence continues to ripple out to this day.

For Paul, the end goal was always people. I want the same to be said of me.

Prayer

Lord, I want to excel at both the macro and the micro visions you have given me. I don't want to sacrifice other people in the name of success. I want to find us all rising together. Give me the vision and energy of Paul to care for the big and the small today. Amen.

Get in the Game

1. Think about the people closest to you. How is your vision influencing them—would they consider it a blessing or a curse? Find specific ways to bless each of them today, be it with time, an encouraging text, meeting a physical need, or something else.

   OR

2. Paul was unafraid to express his emotions toward the people who were closest to him. He called the church in Thessalonica his "glory and joy." Who needs to hear words of love and affirmation from you? Make it happen today.

DAY 47

BOLD ASKS AND BOLD ACTIONS
MEN TAKE MINORITY POSITIONS

> And Peter answered him, "Lord, if it is you, command me to come to you on the water." He said, "Come." So Peter got out of the boat and walked on the water and came to Jesus.
>
> Matthew 14:28–29

This story never ceases to inspire and challenge me.

While many focus on the fact that Peter took his eyes off Jesus and began to sink, that's not the main point for me. Instead, it is the fact that Peter asked and acted. For a few moments, he actually walked on the water like Jesus.

I regularly wonder if I would have been bold enough to get out of the boat or to even ask. Peter took action because he understood the authority of Jesus and wanted an experience. And not just a miraculous experience—he wanted more for his life. In a day and age when we justify our choices, think we are victims, and are satisfied with the status quo, I find Peter's attitude all the more inspiring.

He wanted something different, so he asked. When Jesus said yes, he acted swiftly.

Peter had an experience no one else on earth has had before or since because he was willing to take a risk and look like a fool. There are any number of places this could have gone wrong. Peter might have asked and had to deal with Jesus saying no to his request. Peter might have gotten the green light and stayed in the boat out of fear. He could have climbed onto the water and immediately sunk. Even for an experienced fisherman, there was a risk of drowning during a storm.

The biggest threat to Peter, though, was the pain of missing an opportunity. Passivity kills more potent lives than anything else, and Peter wasn't about to let that happen to him.

What the Bible says is true: "You do not have, because you do not ask" (James 4:2). How many opportunities have I missed because I wasn't bold enough to ask? Where have I let passivity silence me? Have I asked expectantly, ready to act, or have I been asking half-heartedly?

Many Christians believe we need to stop asking and expecting more from God because there are other people more in need of his blessing and presence—as if we were all living in an orphanage and God only has so much gruel to go around. Not true.

In the entire Bible, no one is ever repelled by God for asking for anything. He may say "no" or "not yet," but he never minds the ask. You won't be punished for wanting more. It is a minority position to slot yourself under the power and authority of God, asking for what you need (and want) in faith, like a child asking a parent. God often rewards those humble enough to do so.

When you ask, be ready to act. It just might be your time to walk on water.

Prayer

Jesus, I am pushed by the faith of Peter to ask and then to act. Thank you for saying yes to his request, and thank you for all the yeses you have given me. I don't want to miss out on more because I was too proud to make the ask. I will be doing that today, and I will be ready to act. Amen.

Get in the Game

1. What do you need to be bold enough to ask God for? If you have never asked, or if you have asked a hundred times, do it again this morning. Even if his answer is no, he will be honored by the level of trust you place in him just by asking.

   OR

2. Peter was primed to act, so when Jesus said yes, he was ready to move. If God says yes to your biggest and boldest request, will you be ready to act? If not, what do you need to change to be better prepared? Do that today as an act of faith. No matter God's answer, I believe he is pleased with your aggressive stance.

DAY 48

THE TEAM ABROAD
MEN ARE TEAM PLAYERS

> I therefore, a prisoner for the Lord, urge you to walk in a manner worthy of the calling to which you have been called, with all humility and gentleness, with patience, bearing with one another in love, eager to maintain the unity of the Spirit in the bond of peace.
>
> Ephesians 4:1–3

Last year, on a trip to Germany, I had the chance to retrace the footsteps of Martin Luther. The sixteenth-century Reformer is a titan of church history. While he is famous for kick-starting the Protestant Reformation, leading to a split in the worldwide Catholic church, that actually wasn't his goal.

As a monk, Luther saw mistakes and abuses in the church. In humility, he attempted to call them to the attention of the authorities. While some want to portray his nailing of the Ninety-Five Theses to the church door in Wittenberg as an act of defiance, it was anything but. The church doors were like the community's bulletin board. He was looking to have an honest discussion about things he couldn't understand or reconcile.

Like Paul before him, Luther wanted to keep the bond of peace. Leaders in the church didn't take kindly to his questions. Great upheaval and turmoil would follow, but so would the rebirth of a movement that had lost its moorings. Modern-day Catholics and Protestants are both the better for it.

There is an example here for all of us to follow. If you count yourself among the followers of Christ, you are part of a team much larger than yourself. It spans every continent and every country in every age of the world.

Unfortunately, the church is known more for drawing dividing lines than it is for being "eager to maintain the unity of the Spirit." It's better known for pride, judgmentalism, and culture wars than humility, gentleness, and patience. On top of it all, we're oftentimes at our worst with each other.

It is a shame how divided the people of God are. If we were united and headed in the same direction, it would be stunning how quickly our world would change. Our differences would be seen as a strength rather than a weakness. Instead, we bicker, debate, fight, and criticize one another, when we could be working together to bring God's love and ways wherever we go.

We are not to share the interpersonal pettiness that the rest of the world thrives on. We are called to be totally united with the rest of Christ's followers. There is a team abroad, and we belong to it.

I am thankful for the life of Luther, and I am thankful for believers of all stripes, Catholic and Protestant, who push my life forward. I've developed a friendship with a Catholic priest who is one of the rare guests to have been on my podcast, *The Aggressive Life*, more than once. We dress differently and we don't believe the same about everything, but we are on the same team. He is a good man who I am honored to call a brother.

You have teammates around the world who don't look like you, speak like you, think like you, live like you, or worship like you. Yet they still bend their knee to the same God.

Unity in the church, learning to cheer on the team abroad, just might be the thing that gets the most attention and does the most good for the hurting world around us.

Prayer

Father, I recognize that you are not only my Father but you also have children in churches big and small, of all worship and teaching styles, on every continent on earth. Thank you for including me in such a wide and diverse family. I will pursue unity today to honor you. Amen.

Get in the Game

1. Ask God if there are any strained relationships with other believers that you need to reconcile. If he puts anyone on your mind, take action today to pursue unity. Relationships are a two-way street, so all you need to worry about is being obedient to God. The other party's response is on them.

    OR

2. Do something to show unity with other believers today. It could be as simple as sending an encouraging text to a friend, as complex as visiting a different church over the weekend, or as far-reaching as looking into the plight of Christians in persecuted parts of the world and committing to pray for them. Whatever you do, be reminded today just how wide the family of God is.

DAY 49

BAYW
MEN WORK

> [Jesus] saw two boats by the lake, but the fishermen had
> gone out of them and were washing their nets. Getting into
> one of the boats, which was Simon's, he asked him to put
> out a little from the land. . . . He said to Simon, "Put out into
> the deep and let down your nets for a catch." And Simon
> answered, "Master, we toiled all night and took nothing! But
> at your word I will let down the nets."
>
> Luke 5:2–5

Peter is getting ready to have one of the strangest days of
work in his entire career. So strange, it will change the tra-
jectory of everything else that comes after it.

If Peter knows anything, it is fishing. He grew up in a fishing community, and it had likely been his apprenticed trade
since late boyhood. Hours and hours upon the water had
given him physical skills that Jesus, who grew up in a building community, didn't have.

Peter is packing up to go home when Jesus approaches and asks him to go back out onto the water. I can see the skeptical look on Peter's face. After working all night and catching nothing, fishing is the last thing he wants to do.

He probably doesn't place great confidence in the counsel of Jesus in regard to fishing, but God is looking to see if Peter will pass the BAYW test: "but at your word."

Whenever God wants us to do something we don't understand or even agree with, he is looking for men who will say "but at your word" and then plow forward. God doesn't reward people who mentally agree with him. He rewards those who actually do what he says.

Research shows that over the course of a lifetime, the average person will spend about 90,000 hours at work. That equals nearly one-third of our entire lives.[1] We are likely to consider how Jesus's words may influence our actions at home or in our finances or in our closest friendships. But work? He has nothing to say about that because he has never been a trucker or salesman or broker or (fill in the blank), right?

Wrong. Jesus isn't content to stay put. When we begin to take him at his word, we will do things we haven't done before. The more we obey, the more he is encouraged to move in and around us. When we don't take him at his word, he chooses to give words to someone else.

Peter wasn't expecting a miracle. He just made the choice to close the gap between hearing and doing. When he takes Jesus at his word and pushes back out into the water, his faith is rewarded. He hauls in the biggest catch of his life—so many fish they begin to tear his nets from the sheer weight. This has massive financial and spiritual implications for his future.

God isn't looking for thinkers or talkers. He wants doers. At home. With friends. And especially at work.

Prayer

Jesus, you are good to include me in your plans and work. Today, I want to answer "but at your word" to everything you ask of me. I want to be rewarded, even if that means getting back out onto the water when I am tired. I trust you. Amen.

Get in the Game

1. Invite God to meet you in your work today. Look at your calendar and take note of the tasks you have before you. Spend time asking him to bless each one and to give you an opportunity to answer "but at your word" before you clock out. Then go about your day looking for him to show up. When you see it, move on it as quickly as possible to meet him in it.

   OR

2. When working, we can get so focused on the tasks at hand that we miss Jesus's marching orders. Today, practice being intentional about listening. Open your phone's clock app and set three alarms for different times during your day. When the alarm goes off, spend thirty seconds asking Jesus if he has any new orders for you. If you feel a nudge, act on it.

DAY 50

WHEN KINGS DON'T GO TO WAR
MEN ARE PROTECTORS

> In the spring of the year, the time when kings go out to battle, David sent Joab, and his servants with him, and all Israel. And they ravaged the Ammonites and besieged Rabbah. But David remained at Jerusalem.
>
> 2 Samuel 11:1

I am at my best when I'm playing offense, not defense. All of us are naturally pulled toward passivity. The fight to push back against this is what sets relational protectors apart.

David is a true biblical hero, and at the same time he is a flawed man with ups and downs. He is uniquely talented in war and eliminating the enemy. It doesn't jibe with our civilized modern sensibilities, but David was really good at killing—whether as a shepherd boy killing wild beasts, a teenager killing Goliath, or a warrior killing thousands of Philistines. This was the sweet spot of David's kingship.

In the ancient world, spring was the time for war. During the cold and wet winter months, invading marauders would encroach on the land of kings who were passing the time in their palaces, castles, or citadels. In the spring, when the ground dried up, the kings would take out their chariots and armies to reclaim the land that was rightfully theirs.

This spring, for whatever reason, David decides to send others to do his work for him. This choice starts a pattern of passivity that will eventually get him into big trouble. If you know the story, you know that the mighty king of Israel will seduce his friend's wife, sleep with her, and then rig a military battle to ensure the friend is killed to cover up his mistake. Ouch.

Part of David's role as king would have been initiating a written history of his kingdom. Everything that entered the official record would have to be approved by him. The reason we even know about this major failure is because he commissioned it to be written down. Why? So we could learn a lesson that stretches over generations: passivity always leads to death. This is especially true in relationships.

David should have been on the battlefield. He was uniquely gifted for war, and it was his duty as king. When he stayed home, he had time for his eyes to wander and to get in trouble. When he seduced his friend's wife, he vastly devalued the worth of both members of that marriage and their commitment to each other. When he tried to cover it up, he put the wrong actions in the wrong place. Passivity created a mess that would take a long time to clean up. Though he eventually received forgiveness, David never fully recovered in terms of his leadership and overall fruitfulness.

The point here isn't to stop you from killing your friend and stealing his wife (though that's always a bad idea). The lesson is that perpetual defense leads to passivity. If you aren't taking new ground, you are losing it.

Whether in your marriage or with friends, in your relationship with your parents or your children, you can't afford to stop playing relational offense. There are times and seasons for defense, but protectors don't just sit at home behind stone walls. They push forward. They keep pursuing. They beat back the marauders of boredom and bad habits, past mistakes and passivity, to take back the land that is rightfully theirs.

Relational protectors understand that connectedness matters. They play offense when it comes to relationships because cruise control never takes us where we want to be.

Prayer

God, I am thankful that David chose to record this history even though it makes him look bad. I will learn from his mistakes. I want to play offense when it comes to the relationships you have given me and the ones you have yet to reveal. Amen.

Get in the Game

1. Think over your relationships—family, friends, at work, and beyond. Where is passivity lulling you into playing a safe defense? Go to war against that today. Do something to invest in a relationship and get to playing some offense. This is what relational protectors do.

   OR

2. David was uniquely gifted for war, but passivity had him staying at home. Spend a few minutes asking God to reveal your unique giftings to you—the skills or attributes that come easily, bring success, and influence others. When you have an idea what those are, consider if you are leveraging them as a protector or not. If yes, then do something today to keep pushing forward. If not, find a way to use your giftings to build relationships around you. Don't stay home when it's time for war.

WEEK
11

DAY 51

DROP THE WEIGHT
MEN HAVE A VISION

> The LORD will fulfill his purpose for me;
> your steadfast love, O LORD, endures forever.
> Do not forsake the work of your hands.
>
> Psalm 138:8

I OD'd on the word *purpose* many years ago. I got so sick of all the hand-wringing from people who couldn't "find their purpose," but it still rubbed off on me. I turned inward, looking to discover something about myself that would unlock God's grand plan for my life. The one true plan that was my purpose.

All that navel-gazing did was lead me to an unending avalanche of doubt and questions: Was I in the right occupation? Was I at the right church? Was I raising my kids the right way? Was there some new business or nonprofit God had destined me to start? Was one of the neighborhood kids destined to be the next Billy Graham and was it on me to find and disciple them? Was I hitting every mark God had placed before me?

There's a better way. No one can live under the oppressive weight of thinking there is some ultimate assignment you have to discover and fulfill or else your life is substandard—or worse, the kingdom of God gets stunted.

Maybe the most significant Bible study I have ever done is Henry Blackaby's *Experiencing God*. I first went through it twenty-five years ago, and it is still bearing fruit in my life. It can all be summed up in one thought: look for what God is already doing and go join him in it.

This is exactly how Jesus lived (John 5:19). If even the Messiah didn't do things on his own initiative and power, why do I think that I can? Dreaming up vision statements and lists of goals has always been a pretty fruitless endeavor for me unless those lists are based on things I already see God clearly doing. In that case, there is momentum that is already being created and I just need to jump in.

If you're having trouble articulating a grand vision for your life, take a deep breath and drop the weight. It is God's job to make sure his purposes are completed. It is our job to jump in and join him in whatever he is already doing.

Prayer

God, you are faithful and true. I am sorry for the times when I shoulder expectations and responsibilities that only you can carry. I trust you to fulfill your purposes for my life. I am on the lookout for how I can join you in that today, and I am ready to move. Amen.

Get in the Game

1. You prayed it, now it's time to do it. Go about your day looking for something that God is already doing around you. When you see it, jump in. If you aren't sure, jump in anyway.

      OR

2. God has given you skills to use in service to him and others. What skills or gifts do you have? Who do you know that could benefit from them? Figure out a way to bless that person with your skill today. This could be the first step on a path to a much larger purpose.

DAY 52

BUCK WILD
MEN TAKE MINORITY POSITIONS

> In those days also I saw the Jews who had married women of Ashdod, Ammon, and Moab. And half of their children spoke the language of Ashdod, and they could not speak the language of Judah. . . . And I confronted them and cursed them and beat some of them and pulled out their hair. And I made them take an oath in the name of God, saying, "You shall not give your daughters to their sons, or take their daughters for your sons or for yourselves."
>
> Nehemiah 13:23–25

I never learned this verse in Sunday school. I don't think Jesus would approve of Nehemiah's methods, but before we let ourselves feel spiritually superior, we need to at least recognize that he isn't dicking around when it comes to trying to honor God.

Marriage is holy and sacred. When a man and woman join in marriage, they become one before God. It is a mystery that represents how God weds himself to us, never to leave us or forsake us. This is why God is very explicit about marriages being equally yoked—meaning both partners trust, submit to, and follow Jesus, or both partners have zero interest in Jesus. We become like our spouse and they become like us. Marry someone you want to pursue Christ with and become more like.

In ancient Israel, God explicitly set the expectation that his people, the Jews, were not to intermarry with any other people groups. This was not a racially or ethnically motivated choice but a spiritual one. God knew the devotion of his people was easily swayed. When given the choice between worshiping him or giving their affections to the false gods of the people groups living around them, they would always falter.

After his violent outburst, Nehemiah goes on to explain to the people that this is exactly what led to the downfall of David's son Solomon. Despite being the richest and wisest king in Israel's history, his reign fell apart because of the influence of foreign wives who pushed him to worship idols. The people haven't learned their lesson and once again have fallen into the same hole.

There isn't anything for us to physically replicate in the way Nehemiah reacts. It is not a good idea to beat anybody or pull their hair out for their marriage choice. But before our modern sensitivities get the best of us, we should ask ourselves, "Am I comfortable with my sin?"

It's a minority position to even use the *S* word anymore, but God doesn't shy away from it. Anything that steals our affections from him is sin. Any mistake that separates us from him is sin. Anything good that we know to do but leave undone is sin.

Nehemiah went buck wild against the blatant sin he encountered. We need that attitude, not for an unbelieving world that lives by a different set of standards but for ourselves. Like the ancient Jews, we are the people of God, created to stand out in the world. If our lives aren't different sexually, financially, relationally, and holistically, then something is wrong with us.

The Jews had grown comfortable with living life in a way that broke the instructions of God and ignored the truth of their past. I must not make that same mistake.

We need an all-out offensive against the sin and rebellion that plague our lives. *Lord, is there anything I need to eliminate from my life? I will gladly put it on the chopping block for you today.*

Prayer

God, I want you to be the center of my attention and affections today. If there is anything competing with your rightful place in my life, let me know and I will move it out of the top spot. I am serious about my sin and stamping it out—not for self-help but to honor you. Amen.

Get in the Game

1. Ask God if there is anything in your life stealing your attention or affections away from him. Spend two minutes in silence listening for a response. If a thought enters your mind, assume it's from him and act on it. How can you turn down the volume of that thing in your life today and give more attention to God?

   OR

2. There are times when we all need the help of a Nehemiah. If you have a sin that is particularly hard for you to conquer, tell a trusted brother about it. Ask him to pray for you and to hold your feet to the fire. It is your responsibility to be vulnerable and honest and to ask for help when you need it.

DAY 53

A BROTHER'S ROLE
MEN ARE TEAM PLAYERS

Then the LORD said to Cain, "Where is Abel your brother?"
He said, "I do not know; am I my brother's keeper?"

Genesis 4:9

Cain and Abel were the first two children born to Adam
and Eve. After their parents' disobedience and expulsion
from the garden of Eden, it didn't take long for things to go
from bad to worse.

Only four chapters into the entire Bible, Cain commits the
first murder, killing his brother. God calls him on the carpet,
and Cain's response of deflection is just as indicative of an
unhealthy heart as the actual murder. Selfish hearts live like
they are responsible for their own health and no one else's.
When faced with a difficult question, the hard-hearted will
respond just as Cain did—answering a question with another question to shift the blame.

To answer Cain's question, YES! In truth, we are our brother's keeper. God hasn't placed us in teams for us to continue operating as isolated orphans. Team members work together. They care for each other. They watch out for each other. They have hard conversations when needed. They mourn together, celebrate together, and compete together.

This is true for every team, from your family to your work pod to your group of friends.

The early-church missionary, Paul, takes this idea and ramps it up a notch. In Galatians 6, he writes:

> Brothers, if anyone is caught in any transgression, you who are spiritual should restore him in a spirit of gentleness. Keep watch on yourself, lest you too be tempted. Bear one another's burdens, and so fulfill the law of Christ. (vv. 1–2)

A brother's responsibility doesn't stop at just being a keeper; a brother is also a restorer. This may sound straightforward, but it is not easy.

It isn't comfortable to give straight talk to a friend in a way that is honest and at the same time gentle. The point isn't just to have a conversation; it is the restoration of a humble walk with God. When we are transgressing, there is a cloak of sin over our life that makes it difficult for us to hear and apply God's truth. We need brothers who will call us out and woo us back.

Left to our natural selfish ways, most of us would rather live and let live. We think, "Doesn't the Bible say 'do unto others'? I wouldn't want anyone in my business, so I won't get into theirs." In the process, we all grow weaker spiritually because we all need and depend upon each other. I must not fall prey to this temptation of not being spiritually engaged. It only leads to an anemic life, anemic relationships, and anemic spirituality.

I am my brother's keeper and my brother's restorer. And so are you.

Prayer

Lord, I am thankful for the people who have taken the risk and spoken to me about my own shortcomings and sins. On this side of it, I am grateful for the boldness and grace they showed to me. Restoration is a beautiful thing. If there is anyone I need to restore today, I am in. Amen.

Get in the Game

1. Nobody gets up in the morning wanting to have a restoration conversation, but it is what the best teammates do. Spend time asking God if there is anyone you need to restore today. If he puts someone on your mind, plan to broach the subject with grace and truth. If no one comes to mind, spend the day reflecting on your own state. Is there anything that bubbles to the surface that you need to get rid of, adjust, or add? Do it today.

   OR

2. Take the initiative and ask a godly man you respect to be your keeper and restorer. Give him permission to observe your life and call you on the carpet if (and when) he notices anything outside the character of Jesus. Be sharpened by his wisdom, words, and correction. He is making you better.

DAY 54

SUCCESS TO BLESS
MEN WORK

> Joseph went in and told Pharaoh, "My father and my brothers, with their flocks and herds and all that they possess, have come from the land of Canaan. They are now in the land of Goshen." . . . And [Joseph's brothers] said to Pharaoh, "Your servants are shepherds, as our fathers were." . . . Then Pharaoh said to Joseph, . . . "The land of Egypt is before you. Settle your father and your brothers in the best of the land. Let them settle in the land of Goshen, and if you know any able men among them, put them in charge of my livestock."
>
> Genesis 47:1, 3, 5–6

A wide-reaching and persistent famine has brought Joseph's family to Egypt. Looking to ensure their well-being and secure a future for the people of God, Joseph makes a masterful move. He presents his family to Pharaoh, purposefully highlighting their skill at shepherding.

Joseph knows that the Egyptians have an aversion to sheep and shepherds, considering the animals dirty and their keepers outcast from normal society. And he knows that Pharaoh has his own livestock that are integral to his wealth and power.

Joseph makes a gamble that pays off. Pharaoh wants separation from the Israelites because of their sheep, but he also wants to ensure they have good land so they can take care of his livestock for him. He agrees to give Joseph's family a huge cut of some of the best land in Egypt. Goshen was green and fertile, with adequate space for crops, livestock, and God's nation to grow under the nose (and protection) of Egypt.

Pharaoh, the most powerful man in the world, gets outmaneuvered by a former slave. Joseph has a brilliant mind for business and success coupled with a depth of spiritual maturity. God uses this combination to bring blessing upon blessing to those in his orbit.

I am in awe of Joseph's foresight, and it leaves me wondering: why are there so few Josephs in the world today? I know people who have spiritual insights but can't figure out how to make money. I know people who are smart enough to make money but have zero spiritual potency and live bankrupt when it comes to faith.

I think we have overreacted to the health and wealth heresy. Believers are overly cynical toward anyone with business savvy and monetary means. Yet those traits don't stop God from using Joseph. In fact, they place Joseph in just the right position to make a major impact. Maybe the work of God would be more vibrant in our land if those of us who know God also had the influence that comes when we have and make money.

When God wants a big task done, he uses people who have proven themselves faithful. Joseph did this. He benefited the entire nation of Egypt by interpreting Pharaoh's dreams and warning of an oncoming famine. Then he led the national food-saving program to ensure everyone would have sustenance through the darkest days. All the while, Joseph greatly increased Pharaoh's wealth by acquiring land and livestock in exchange for grain.

Joseph stewarded his life well, and God gave him an opportunity to use his skills to bless his own family and generations to follow.

Let's stop looking at success and business acumen as a sign that someone is spiritually shallow or outside the will of God. In fact, it might be just the opposite. We need more men following the example of Joseph: Work hard. Pursue success. Bless others.

Prayer

Father, I apologize for assuming that loserliness is next to godliness. This was not the case for Joseph. Whether I find overt success or not, I will remain committed to you. May my work ethic today bring a smile to your face. Amen.

Get in the Game

1. Do you ask God to bless you with success in your work? Take time to consider what success at work today would look like, then ask God specifically for that. Whether he answers your prayer or not, I believe he is pleased that you are leaning on him. Keep working hard and pushing forward.

   OR

2. Joseph's success blessed everyone around him. This is a posture we can assume no matter our salary. At work today, find a way to bless others: buy a coworker a coffee, bring donuts to the office, or take time to encourage your teammates in front of others. Choose to elevate others above yourself and see how it influences your environment.

DAY 55

SEEING PAST BLINDNESS
MEN ARE PROTECTORS

A ruler asked him, "Good Teacher, what must I do to inherit eternal life?" And Jesus said to him, . . . "You know the commandments: 'Do not commit adultery, Do not murder, Do not steal, Do not bear false witness, Honor your father and mother.'" And he said, "All these I have kept from my youth." When Jesus heard this, he said to him, "One thing you still lack. Sell all that you have and distribute to the poor, and you will have treasure in heaven; and come, follow me." But when he heard these things, he became very sad, for he was extremely rich.

Luke 18:18–23

Jesus's famous interaction with the rich young ruler is one that many people misunderstand. Am I to liquidate everything I own and give the money away? Maybe. But I actually don't think this is a story about Jesus wanting us to be possessionless. Instead, it is a story about a person who lacks spiritual self-awareness and how money can blind us.

This young man actually believes he has perfectly kept the Ten Commandments, God's rules for righteous living handed down to Moses thousands of years earlier. No one in the history of Israel, except for Jesus, could have made that claim. Yet this young man actually believes he's done it.

Jesus gives him a challenge that reveals his spiritual blindness. When the young man cannot pull the trigger, the blinders fall off. He sees that he isn't as pure as he thinks he is. He loves money, power, prestige, and the things that come with them more than he loves God. When we are unwilling to give something away, it owns us instead of God owning us.

This money blindness still exists today. A common affliction for people who are rich is that we become deluded that our ideas are the right ideas and that we are the smartest in the room. I have interacted with people who have many more zeros behind their net worth than I do. It always amazes me how, even though these people haven't been following Christ as long as I have, haven't been to seminary, and have never led a volunteer organization, they seem to think that their ideas should win the day.

We fall into the same trap as this young man: money makes it easier to think more highly of ourselves than we ought. Money makes admitting that we have needs—or even seeing our needs—very difficult. Money can blind us from seeing that we are actually rich.

Rich people get paid even when they don't work. Rich people buy new shoes before the last pair wears out. Rich people buy clothes not to survive or keep warm but to look fashionable. Rich people need closets, basements, and garages to store things they rarely use. In other words, many of us are deluded rich people.

Having too much can be blinding, but so can having too little.

As a child, I remember getting the fewest and cheapest presents compared to my neighbor friends. In college, I remember not being able to afford toilet paper and having to sell my car because I couldn't keep gas in it. As newlyweds, stifling credit card debt caused my new wife and I to have to move back in with her parents. We became new parents ourselves because we couldn't afford birth control. When my daughter was due, we didn't have insurance and the hospital took us on as "charity care."

Scarcity creates a type of blindness where we believe that there will never be enough, that everything depends on us, and that money is the problem. Not so. The Bible warns about the love of money left to run rampant (1 Tim. 6:10), but it also says that God gives us the ability to build wealth

(Deut. 8:18), that diligent hard work leads to paydays (Prov. 10:4), and that those with extra income should use it to bless others and spend some to enjoy their life (1 Tim. 6:17–18).

Jesus spent a lot of time teaching about money because it is one of the biggest barriers to accessing the life God has for us—either too much of it or too little. Unlike the rich young ruler, Jesus actually did become poor for our sakes (2 Cor. 8:9). He left the riches of heaven to come to our impoverished world in order to serve.

Financial protectors throw off money blindness to properly see reality. They make money to help meet needs. They give money back to God and to others to show that it doesn't own them. They save money for the future. And they spend money to bring joy to life. These are biblical disciplines based on the wisdom of God, and they work.

This young man might have been rich in possessions, but he was living blind. The first step to becoming financial protectors is to see. Let's be better than he was.

Prayer

God, I don't want to live blind. Where I am, shift my vision so that I can see clearly. I want to be a financial protector for those who depend on me. Everything I have originates with you, and I am willing to use my resources in whatever way you prompt me today. Amen.

Get in the Game

1. Read Matthew 20:29–34. If you are ready to throw off money blindness, make the same ask as these two men: "Lord, let our eyes be opened." Spend time in prayer, asking God for clarity around any blind spots you have about finances. Then spend time listening. Whatever God nudges you about, act on it as quickly as possible.

   OR

2. Financial protectors make money, give money, save money, and spend money. Which of these is the hardest for you? Do something today that will begin to build strength in that area. If saving is hard, skip the coffee on the way to work and move that five dollars over to your savings account. If making money is hard, sell something you have on Facebook Marketplace. Be willing to get uncomfortable and throw off money blindness.

WEEK 12

DAY 56

SERVANTS FIRST
MEN HAVE A VISION

> We are the servants of the God of heaven and earth, and
> we are rebuilding the house that was built many years ago,
> which a great king of Israel built and finished.
>
> Ezra 5:11

In a world punch-drunk on individualism, personal accomplishment, and fame, the Bible's wisdom stands in stark contrast: vision trumps identity all day, every day. Your normal day job can be done in such a way as to put vision into action as you serve your God.

We don't know the names of these men risking their lives to rebuild the temple of God in Jerusalem, because that's not what is most important to them. Instead, they were "servants of the God of heaven and earth," and they are aligned with his purposes. Nothing could get in their way. But that doesn't mean people didn't try.

After seventy years of exile in Babylon, God's people had finally been allowed to return to their homeland. Yet the temple remained in ruins as the people focused on their homes, farms, and businesses first. When construction on the temple did begin, it was met with an endless stream of scoffers, detractors, and enemies.

A particularly nasty pair, governors of a nearby province, wrote a letter to King Darius in Babylon to tattle on the Jews. They hoped he would use his power to permanently end the building project. When those governors approached the builders and asked for their names, they answered with the bold proclamation in Ezra 5:11.

Rather than an attempt to sidestep trouble with the king, I believe their response was a challenge to the troublemakers. They essentially said, "It doesn't matter who we are. What matters is that we are following the God who made everything, including you. Your selfish will and your lowly power mean nothing to us."

Thousands of years later, I still get a jolt from reading this passage. The individual identities of these men are lost to history, but their vision is not. Our culture might preach self-fulfillment, but only the eternal visions of God will last. I know where I want to put my time and effort.

This is a good reminder for me that, more than being a pastor, husband, father, friend, or any other title life may lay on me, I must be a servant of God first.

My identity isn't in my name, my accomplishments, or my aspirations. I am a servant willing to do whatever my Master wants done. That is my vision.

Prayer

Father, you are my King and I want to serve you diligently. Show me how I have made my visions about myself and give me wisdom for how to correct that. Give me work to do and I will complete it today. Amen.

Get in the Game

1. Servants are ready and willing to move, with no regard for their own social standing or perception. Today, find a way to serve someone else whom society might consider "beneath you," knowing that we are all on equal footing before God.

   OR

2. We all feel a pull to focus on ourselves. Find a way to cut against that today. If social media gives you a dopamine hit of importance, shut it down for twenty-four hours. If you are putting too much pride in your position at work, stay late and clean out the workroom. If you feel secure because of the money in your savings account, make a donation to a nonprofit. Whatever helps you come against your own self-importance is a good exercise in being a servant.

DAY 57

UP FOR AWKWARD
MEN TAKE MINORITY POSITIONS

> The LORD said, "I will surely return to you about this time
> next year, and Sarah your wife shall have a son." And Sarah
> was listening at the tent door behind him. Now Abraham
> and Sarah were old, advanced in years. The way of women
> had ceased to be with Sarah. So Sarah laughed to herself,
> saying, "After I am worn out, and my lord is old, shall I have
> pleasure?"
>
> Genesis 18:10–12

Take minority positions and I can guarantee you will find
yourself in awkward situations. Push through them anyway.
Blessing may lie on the other side. Just ask Abraham and
Sarah.

God chooses an old, childless couple to be the center
point of his plan for humanity. He promises Abraham and
Sarah that they will have a child, and this child will grow
into a great nation that blesses the entire world.

When Sarah overhears the news here in Genesis 18, she laughs out of disbelief. You can't blame her. She lays out the evidence pretty clearly—so much so, it may make some of us cringe.

At one hundred and ninety years old respectively, Abraham likely doesn't have the "swimmers" he once did, and Sarah is dried up, decades past her childbearing years. She even asks herself, "Shall I have pleasure?" alluding both to the fact that they hadn't had sex in a long time (because they couldn't), as well as the pleasure of finally having a child after waiting her entire life.

On paper, there is no way Abraham and Sarah are going to be able to conceive a child, let alone carry one full-term and give birth. But they go forward anyway. God's plans are sometimes outlandish and beyond our reach. If we depend upon our own ability (or virility or fertility), we will never be able to reach the finish line. He alone is the X factor, and he is worth the risk.

Here is the thing no one ever talks about when it comes to Abraham and Sarah: this was not an immaculate conception. God didn't plant the baby in Sarah's womb like he did with Mary. That means Abraham and Sarah had to get back into the bedroom and go to work. It may seem sacrilegious to think about it, but the text of Genesis 17 and 18 screams for us to consider it.

God made a promise. He would fulfill it, but Abraham and Sarah still had a part to play. I wonder what they were like heading into the bedroom. Were they giddy? Nervous? Expectant? Worried if they still had the ability or stamina? Were they awkward and out of practice? The answers to those questions don't really matter. They moved forward in faithfulness anyway, and the world has never been the same.

God still calls people to do things others will consider ridiculous. No one is too old—or too young—for minority positions.

If it means experiencing God, I'll embrace the awkwardness every single time.

Prayer

God, your plans are well beyond anything I could imagine or dream of. I want the good things you have for me, even if it means having to weather periods of awkwardness, hard work, or even doubt. You are the focus of my day today. I am up for whatever you want to do. Amen.

Get in the Game

1. Think back over the last few years. Is there a time you really stretched yourself to chase something God put on your radar—when you did something others considered foolish or ridiculous?

   - If yes, consider what you learned through that scenario. How did it form your faith? Are you still taking such substantial risks?

   - If no, think through what factors kept you from moving. How can you minimize their influence and impact in your life now? What is the larger lesson to be learned so next time you answer "yes"?

   OR

2. Ephesians 3:20 describes God as "him who is able to do immeasurably more than all we ask or imagine" (NIV). Spend a few minutes engaging your imagination. If the tap of God's blessing was turned on full blast in your life, what would it look like? What would be the state of your relationships? Your finances? Your work? Your fun? When you are finished, ask God for those things. No matter how he answers, I think he is pleased that you recognize him as the source of all good things.

DAY 58

QUICK HITTERS
MEN ARE TEAM PLAYERS

> Love one another with brotherly affection. Outdo one another in showing honor. . . . Live in harmony with one another.
>
> Romans 12:10, 16

It is easy to look at all that Paul accomplished in his life and assume it was because of his type A personality. There is no doubt he was driven. He traveled the Middle East for years, planting churches, investing in leaders, and spreading the good news of Jesus. But he wasn't a lone ranger who torched people—he didn't use people for his mission, people were the mission!

As we read Paul's letters, it becomes obvious that he had deep relational bonds. At the end of Romans, he namechecks twenty-nine different people and their families for personal greetings. Most of us can't name the last person we spent time with who wasn't part of our family or office, and the average American can't name their five closest neighbors.

When Paul left Ephesus after building into people there, the leaders wept at the thought of him not being with them any longer (Acts 20:38). Many leaders we know leave the room and their people weep for joy. Some believers I interact with give me nothing emotionally, spiritually, or relationally. They are empty cisterns who have nothing to pour into others. I'm not sure if it's because they have nothing to give or want to give nothing. On the other hand, there is Paul, who loves people with abandon and affection, resulting in harmony.

We can learn a lot from Paul about being a team player. In Romans 12, he drops a barrage of one-two punches to help us live well with other people. We realize we should "love one another," but how? Here are a couple of quick hitters:

1. *Be affectionate.* It is one thing to be physically affirming with your spouse, but most of us struggle to show any kind of affection to our friends beyond a handshake or fist bump. We never got past the awkward middle school stage. We can do better than that. Take a risk and give a hug. Pray for someone with your hand on their shoulder. Roughhouse like brothers. Touch is critical for relational well-being.

2. *Show honor.* Instead of competing with one another along the lines of career success and physical fitness, what if we excelled in honoring and exalting each other? For some reason it is easier for me to tease than to encourage. I find it more natural to poke fun at my friends' quirks than to highlight the areas where they outshine me. Culture may exalt criticism and cynicism, but I must be better than that.

3. *Live in harmony.* We make mistakes, we grate on each other, and sometimes we cross lines. Forgiveness is the path to harmony. The Greek word *aphiemi*, translated as "forgive," means "release or let go." Letting go isn't dependent on someone approaching us, owning their mistakes, and formally apologizing. It is a decision we make for our own spiritual sanity and harmony with others. Releasing things so bitterness doesn't fill our heart keeps us spiritually nimble and agile.

Teams are as good and as healthy as their individual players. Focus on these quick hitters today and you will elevate the status of every team you belong to.

Prayer

God, thank you for the reminder from Paul that people are the mission. No matter what I have on the docket for today, I want to be a team player who is affectionate, shows honor, and lives in harmony with my teammates. This is relational wisdom I want to see elevate my teams. Amen.

Get in the Game

1. Of Paul's three quick hitters above, which one sticks out as an area of potential growth for you? Spend time considering how you can put it into action today. Whether it's choosing forgiveness from a past hurt, purposefully elevating coworkers at the office, or being more affectionate with your kids, know that God is honored by your initiative.

    OR

2. Can't name the last person you spent time with who wasn't part of your family or office? Fix that relational gap today. Get in touch with a friend and put something on the calendar in the next seven days that will get you face-to-face time. Then stick to it.

DAY 59

FAITHFUL TO FRUITFUL
MEN WORK

> In the morning, as he was returning to the city, [Jesus] became hungry. And seeing a fig tree by the wayside, he went to it and found nothing on it but only leaves. And he said to it, "May no fruit ever come from you again!" And the fig tree withered at once.
>
> Matthew 21:18–19

This story throws a wrench into the image of Jesus as a Frisbee-throwing hippie on a mission to preach love and good vibes. Jesus was hungry. Then he was angry. A tree withers as a result.

Jesus really cares about fruit, but not in a physical hunger sort of way. He is deeply concerned about what our lives are producing. He is looking to see if we are taking actions that lead to good results out of a heart to honor him.

Jesus gets angry when the tree looks healthy or leafy but doesn't have anything of substance or sustenance to offer.

It makes him just as angry when our lives look spiritual but aren't having a tangible impact beyond producing more leaves.

I can look good and leafy by going to church, completing this devotional book, and staying away from obvious public sins, but that doesn't necessarily mean I'm producing fruit that satisfies Jesus. I can make myself look real leafy on Instagram or on Sunday mornings or even in the office, but that doesn't say anything about my quickness to obey God's promptings, take the risks he puts in front of me, or sacrifice for others. Wearing a Christian T-shirt is fine, but it can also be a showing of leafiness by a person who has never borne the fruit of praying with someone to receive Christ.

I don't know the last time you tried to grow something, but we shouldn't miss this fact: fruit grows slowly. Sometimes painfully so.

A financial adviser on my podcast recently said, "The best way to build wealth is consistent savings over time."[1] Sounds too simple and too difficult at the same time. We love the thought of overnight success or going viral. Life doesn't work that way in any arena.

We go forward in life by taking small, deliberate, and consistent steps. Fruit, both physical and spiritual types, grows with small daily deposits. We build muscle mass by hitting the gym three to four times a week, not after one workout. Daily time with God over decades, not a weekend, is the key to spiritual depth. Relationships grow rich in intimacy from years of persistent sacrifice, vulnerability, and fun.

I must deny the modern lie that good things come to those who wait. No, good things come to those who do the small things over time.

One day Jesus will push aside the leaves of our life and look for one thing: fruit. It is true that men work, but our biggest efforts should be focused on the people, projects, and initiatives that will last.

Jesus cares more about the money I gave to my church than my salary or 401(k) status. He cares more about my being present for my children than the number of employees who report to me. He cares more about growing love, joy, peace, and patience inside me than how many things I can check off my to-do list today.

Fruitful people get that way by first being faithful. They put in the reps, and then they reap a harvest.

Men work hard. And they work even harder—and longer—at what produces fruit.

Prayer

Jesus, I don't want to be like the tree that angered you. I don't want a life of good-looking leaves with no fruit. Show me a place where I need to be faithful, to put in more reps, and I will do that today. I want to bear fruit that is pleasing to you. Amen.

Get in the Game

1. In what arena of life are you looking for fruit without putting in the faithful reps? That changes today. Whether it is improving your marriage or your financial situation or incorporating more fun into your life, it's reps over time that make the difference. Restart that process today by taking a step toward your goal. Then do it again tomorrow. And the next day. Fruit is coming.

   OR

2. Read Galatians 5:22–23. Choose one "fruit of the Spirit" to focus on and grow today, then determine how you can put it into practice. You might choose to grow gentleness by caring for the baby when you get home from work, peace by not restarting the argument from last night, or kindness by pulling your neighbor's garbage cans in from the curb. Whatever you do, consider it the first faithful rep in growing more of this fruit in your life.

DAY 60

THE GREAT CLOUD
MEN ARE PROTECTORS

Therefore, since we are surrounded by so great a cloud of witnesses, let us also lay aside every weight, and sin which clings so closely, and let us run with endurance the race that is set before us, looking to Jesus, the founder and perfecter of our faith, who for the joy that was set before him endured the cross, despising the shame, and is seated at the right hand of the throne of God.

Hebrews 12:1–2

As a protector, you are the first line of defense and the first responder. You are a backstop for the people around you. The good news? God hasn't left you without a backstop.

Who are the "cloud of witnesses" in Hebrews 12? Not friends we may worship alongside on a Sunday morning but faithful heroes who have gone before us. They are viewing our choices from heaven right now. This covers every spiritual great, from a grandmother who had a close walk with Christ all the way up to King David, Peter, and Jesus himself.

God puts certain things in the Bible to motivate us in our day-to-day lives. This is one of those motivators for me. The spiritual greats aren't just watching me, they are cheering me on. That's what witnesses do at sporting events, and this passage makes it clear we are running a race right now. It is a race that is difficult and long. It is a race that all the heroes of the faith understand. They ran and they won their race, and they are pushing us to do the same.

It is humbling to think of spiritual heroes rooting for me, but Jesus takes it all up a notch. A few chapters earlier, the writer of Hebrews describes Jesus as indestructible (7:16), the initiator of our hope (7:18–19), and right now interceding to God the Father on our behalf (7:25). Jesus is mentioning my name, my issues, and my needs to God. He is constantly working for my benefit, and he is doing the same thing for you.

Spectators at a sporting event can't play the game for the athletes on the field, but they can absolutely influence it. Go to a playoff game at Lambeau Field, a World Series game at Yankee Stadium, or any game day at the Horseshoe at Ohio State, and you'll see what I mean.

There is a stadium full of spiritual greats rooting for me, with Jesus at the head of the pack. So why do I lack confidence? Why do I sometimes feel like I am on my own? Why do I think it's all up to me? The truth is that I am covered in so many ways, much more than I can even imagine.

When I think of Denny Pattyn, the man who led me to Christ, cheering me on from heaven to keep taking new ground, I find a fresh burst of energy. When I think of Gil Hopkins yelling from the stands for me to stay in the game, I'll push through any pain. He made quite a journey from a tough cop to an old man who had all his joints replaced and rode a scooter. He pushed me and he fathered me for years. He kept this quote by his desk:

> Life's journey is not to arrive at the grave safely, in a well-preserved body, but rather to skid in sideways, totally worn out, shouting, "Holy s***, what a ride!" (Hunter S. Thompson)

When I think of Jacob, the Bible's hustling patriarch, encouraging me to endure, I am motivated to keep moving. When I think of King David shouting his support, I find the strength to get up and try again. When I think of Jesus going to bat for my every need, I find the strength to keep running.

If you have read through this devotional and made it to the last page, know this: you have a spiritual cheering section pushing you to keep going. You have a savior in Jesus, who knows your every need and is working on your behalf. You have a band of brothers that stretches around the world rooting for you. And you have a believer in me.

You are a protector.

You work hard.

You are a team player.

You take minority positions.

You chase visions.

The micro choices you make in these areas are being watched and cheered by the godly men who have gone before you.

You are a man. Keep those shoes tied tight and your muscles primed for movement. In this race, there's still plenty of ground to cover.

Prayer

Jesus, thank you for being my backstop as I protect those around me. Thank you for interceding on my behalf. Thank you for the cloud of witnesses pushing me to keep going. I don't deserve any of this, but I am beyond grateful to be included in your family. I will work to honor that legacy today. Amen.

Get in the Game

1. Close your eyes and imagine the great cloud of witnesses surrounding you. Who would be included? Who is cheering the loudest? Who is pushing you to keep going? Jesus is at the center of it all. Any time you feel tempted to give up today, think about this crowd and keep going.

   OR

2. Go outside and run until you feel fatigued . . . then run a little farther. Let the ache you feel in your muscles remind you that life is a race of endurance that oftentimes includes pains and soreness. After your run, send up a quick prayer to Jesus, thanking him for fighting for you and making any specific requests that come to mind. Your Protector is working, even when you can't see it.

NOW WHAT?

If you've finished this sixty-day journey toward a powerful life, you are in the upper 1 percent of men.

Most men don't make hard commitments because they want to keep their options open.

You buckled in and did something that took more than an afternoon to complete.

Most men feel like a fish out of water when it comes to faith.

You chose to focus on it, building spiritual muscle in the process.

Most men can't remember the last time they prayed.

You did it for sixty days.

Most men prefer intellectual challenges over physical ones.

You not only read this book, you put it into action.

Most men don't have a code that they live by.

You have worked the five marks into your life, day after day after day.

Well done. You are the type of man that God chooses to work through. You are going places and have a bright future.

That being said, none of us ever arrive when it comes to the marks. I didn't write this content because I master all five marks every day. I still find outages and areas where passivity wants to creep in. Growing in the marks and chasing the movement of God is a lifelong pursuit. I hope we cross paths on the road.

If you find yourself wanting more reps when it comes to the marks, here are some good options:

- Start this book again. The devotions are designed to be applicable over multiple reads. I believe God will do something different in you the second (or even third) time through.

- Recognizing a mark where you have space to grow? Do a deep dive. There are twelve entries for each of the marks in this book. Focus on those specific ones over the next period of time and see what God does to grow that mark in your life.

- Get a group of like-minded men together and work through *The Five Marks of a Man Tactical Guide*. Nearly all ancient civilizations initiated their boys into manhood. This action-first guide is designed to escort you down the primal path to courageous manhood. It is a creative, highly designed adventure in which you tear up the book and become a man in the process. Find more information at BrianTome.com/FiveMarks.

- If you haven't yet, pick up the book that started it all: *The Five Marks of a Man*. It provides a deep dive into each of the marks, with personal stories and application I picked up the hard way. Bonus points if you discuss it with other good guys. More information at BrianTome.com/FiveMarks.

Whatever you do, keep pushing forward. Passivity always takes us backward, but healthy aggressiveness will keep you sharp.

I'll see you out there.

NOTES

Day 3 Grab a Shovel

1. Sue Bowman, "Oxen No Has-Beens When It Comes to Hard Pulling," Lancaster Farming, August 24, 2011, https://www.lancasterfarming.com/farming-news/northern _edition/oxen-no-has-beens-when-it-comes-to-hard-pulling/article_b79a5f8f-5d4b -578d-997a-f385095dc7c9.html.

2. Matt and Jessica Hardecke, "What Do Cows Eat?," Clover Meadows Beef, November 21, 2022, https://www.clovermeadowsbeef.com/what-do-cows-eat/.

3. "We Show How Much Animals Poop . . . With Fruit!," Pet Poo Skiddoo, accessed August 23, 2023, https://petpooskiddoo.com/blog/showing-much-animals-poop -fruit/.

Day 8 The Most Important Gift

1. Mary Elizabeth Williams, "Here's Why Experts Say Men Need More Friends in Their Lives—And How They Can Make Them," Salon, June 20, 2023, https://www .salon.com/2023/06/20/heres-why-experts-say-men-need-more-friends-in-their -lives--and-how-they-can-make-them/.

2. Madeline Holcombe, "Why Most Men Don't Have Enough Close Friends," CNN, November 29, 2022, https://www.cnn.com/2022/11/29/health/men-friendships -wellness/index.html.

Day 9 God Is Invested

1. Gallup, "State of the Global Workplace: 2023 Report," Gallup.com, accessed September 1, 2023, https://www.gallup.com/workplace/349484/state-of-the-global-workplace.aspx#ite-506891.

2. Gallup, "State of the Global Workplace."

3. Alexandra Baruffati, "Workplace Distractions Statistics: All You Need to Know," Gitnux Market Data, last updated October 31, 2023, https://blog.gitnux.com/workplace-distractions-statistics/.

4. Gallup, "State of the Global Workplace."

Day 13 A Team That Works

1. Dr. Christopher S. Baird, "How Much Water Can a Camel Store in Its Hump?," Science Questions with Surprising Answers, September 18, 2013, https://www.wtamu.edu/~cbaird/sq/2013/09/18/how-much-water-can-a-camel-store-in-its-hump/.

Day 20 Sights on the Enemy

1. Julia Shapero, "Belief in God, the Devil Falls to New Low: Gallup," The Hill, July 20, 2023, https://thehill.com/changing-america/respect/diversity-inclusion/4107968-belief-in-god-the-devil-falls-to-new-low-gallup/.

Day 23 Well Spent

1. "Life Expectancy in the U.S. Dropped for the Second Year in a Row in 2021," Centers for Disease Control and Prevention, August 31, 2022, https://www.cdc.gov/nchs/pressroom/nchs_press_releases/2022/20220831.htm.

2. "Suicide," National Institute of Mental Health, updated February 2024, https://www.nimh.nih.gov/health/statistics/suicide.

3. "Excessive Alcohol Use Is a Risk to Men's Health," Centers for Disease Control and Prevention, June 2022, https://www.cdc.gov/alcohol/fact-sheets/mens-health.htm.

Day 35 The Chorus of the Comfortable

1. Rev. Dr. Martin Luther King Jr., "Remaining Awake Through a Great Revolution," Oberlin College Archives, accessed August 29, 2023, https://www2.oberlin.edu /external/EOG/BlackHistoryMonth/MLK/CommAddress.html.

Day 43 The Team at Home

1. Daniel De Visé, "Americans Are Waiting Longer and Longer to Get Married," The Hill, June 5, 2023, https://thehill.com/homenews/state-watch/4032467-americans -are-waiting-longer-and-longer-to-get-married/.

2. De Visé, "Americans Are Waiting Longer and Longer to Get Married."

3. Sandra Johnson and Shannon Sabo, "New Census Bureau Population Estimates Show COVID-19 Impact on Fertility and Mortality Across the Nation," United States Census Bureau, March 24, 2022, https://www.census.gov/library/stories/2022/03 /deaths-outnumbered-births-in-half-of-states-between-2020-and-2021.html.

Day 44 Not *For* but *From*

1. Gottlob Schrenk, "εὐδοκέω, εὐδοκία," *Theological Dictionary of the New Testament*, ed. Gerhard Kittel, trans. G. W. Bromiley (Grand Rapids: Eerdmans, 1964), 2:738, Logos Bible Software.

Day 49 BAYW

1. "One Third of Your Life Is Spent at Work," Gettysburg College, accessed September 29, 2023, https://www.gettysburg.edu/news/stories?id=79db7b34-630c -4f49-ad32-4ab9ea48e72b.

Day 59 Faithful to Fruitful

1. "Episode 53: Ben Beshear and John Brannon—LiveWell Capital," *The Aggressive Life with Brian Tome*, podcast, November 3, 2020, https://audioboom.com/posts /7718879-episode-53-ben-beshear-and-john-brannon-livewell-capital.

BRIAN TOME has been leading men for over two decades. Whether it's on an adventure motorcycle over the Rockies or in a boardroom, he knows the power of challenge, brotherhood, and no-nonsense leadership. Brian is a builder who founded and leads Crossroads Church. He's also written five books, hosts *The Aggressive Life* podcast, and started Man Camp, a primitive weekend camping experience that's driven tens of thousands of men to reclaim the code of manhood. Brian spends his free time hunting, camping, or rehabbing a 1978 Jeep CJ-7. He lives with his wife, Libby, in Cincinnati.

Connect with Brian:

www.BrianTome.com

 @BrianDTome   @BrianTome   @BrianTome

For weekly hits of healthy aggression
to keep you moving forward, subscribe
to *The Aggressive Life with Brian Tome* podcast,
available on all major podcast platforms.